P9-CMN-791

THE NAVAHO MISSILE PROJECT

The Story of the "Know-How" Missile of American Rocketry

JAMES N. GIBSON

Schiffer Military/Aviation History
Atglen, PA

Acknowledgements
Joe Pomykata, Navaho Program
Bill Lerna, Navaho Program
Conrad Lueke, Navaho Program
Dale D. Meyers, Navaho Program
John G. Hazard, Navaho Program
Fred Hill, Navaho Program
Vern Goodman, Navaho Program
Alan Bius, Public Relations, Rockwell International
Babs Angel, Public Relations, 45th Space Wing, Patrick AFB
Raymond Puffer, Historian, Edwards AFB
Mark C. Cleary, Chief Historian, 45th Space Wing, Patrick AFB

Special Thanks To
William F. Gibson Jr., Navaho Program
My Father

Book Design by Ian Robertson.

Copyright © 1996 by James N. Gibson.
Library of Congress Catalog Number: 95-72319

All rights reserved. No part of this work may be reproduced or used in any forms or by any means – graphic, electronic or mechanical, including photocopying or information storage and retrieval systems – without written permission from the copyright holder.

Printed in China.
ISBN: 0-7643-0048-2

We are interested in hearing from authors with book ideas on related topics.

Published by Schiffer Publishing Ltd.
77 Lower Valley Road
Atglen, PA 19310
Please write for a free catalog.
This book may be purchased from the publisher.
Please include $2.95 postage.
Try your bookstore first.

Contents

Introduction

The Navaho program is the least known, yet the most important of the United States early missile programs. Like most research efforts, it produced its share of explosions and accidents. It also produced heroic actions, significant aviation firsts, and events that could make your ribs hurt from laughter. Yet the real importance of the Navaho was the technological advances it produced. To put it simply, the Navaho missile was the grandfather of the United States space program and the world's most modern aircraft.

The Navaho program began in 1946, one of several post-war missile research efforts. The goal was to determine if an intercontinental weapon like the German A-9/A-10 New York rocket was possible. In doing this however, the Navaho project produced major advances in every discipline of engineering.

In just ten years this program accomplished several technological firsts. The X-10 test drone was the first turbojet powered vehicle to exceed Mach 2. It also was the first aircraft to fly a complete mission under inertial (computer) guidance. Later, the G-26 ramjet powered vehicle became the first jet aircraft to reach Mach 3 and an altitude of 77,000 feet. Even the Navaho booster engine would set a record by producing 405,000 pounds of thrust: a benchmark that would last for five years.

These accomplishments have escaped public notice for more then three decades due to the program's "Top Secret" classification. Under this classification, publication of the program's accomplishments was illegal while the program was underway. Thus, the first public mention of the program was the news report of its cancellation in July 1957.

The Navaho was canceled for two reasons. First, it encountered minor technical problems producing repeated delays. These delays would earn the missile the derogatory name of "Never-Go-Navaho."

The second and most important reason for the cancellation was the rapid development of the ICBM. Before the Navaho was canceled the first Atlas ICBM was launched. Within a few months of cancellation the Soviet Union launched Sputnik. Thus, before the first production missile could have flown, the Navaho was militarily obsolete.

With ICBMs flying at the end of 1957 no one was interested in talking about a Mach 3 cruise missile. Aviation journals noted its existence and business journals noted the cancellations impact on North American. After that the program slipped into oblivion. Its documents, still bearing the "Secret" stamp, disappeared into government archives. Finally, the two remaining Navaho vehicles went on public display in places were the public rarely goes.

So effective is the Navaho's disappearance that few people today know it existed. Forty years after its cancellation many of its documents are still classified as "Secret." The most pointed example of this is the official U.S. Air Force history of the program which is still under going declassification. Surprisingly, of those documents that have been declassified, most are now listed as "Restricted." Because these documents contain what is called Export Control Data they cannot be viewed by foreign nationals. This also means that the information contained in these documents cannot be published If the book could be read by foreign nationals or sent to a foreign country.

So what is the purpose of this manuscript. Is it to tell people about a missile no one now remembers except old engineers. Is it to talk about a vehicle that set a few records and then was canceled as better vehicles came into being. Is it to identify a strange looking aircraft in the Air Force Museum Annex at Wright-Patterson AFB, or a missile at the Cape Canaveral missile park. Could it even be to lambaste the government for continuing to restrict information on this missile forty years after cancellation.

This book is one person's attempt to state the accomplishments of this program while maintaining the present government restrictions. Though Navaho failed to become a military weapon, it was one of the most productive programs the U.S. ever started. Accomplishments that should now be publicly recognized.

The technology Navaho created is worth more than all the gold in Fort Knox: hence the present restrictions. In rocket technology alone the Navaho made possible the Thor, Jupiter and Redstone missiles. It also allowed the construction of the Atlas ICBM's engines, thus sealing its own fate. In the years to come this engine technology would power the Apollo moon rocket, and our present Space Shuttle.

Electronics was another area enhanced by Navaho technology. The program gave us the airborne digital computer, modular electronic circuitry, and the all inertial navigation system [all axis]. The development of modular [transistorized] circuitry alone revolutionized the electronics industry, improving the reliability and reparability of countless electronic devices.

The Navaho even effected manufacturing. Probably the greatest legacy is Chem-Milling, now used throughout our commercial aerospace industry for the manufacturing of aircraft body panels. Automatic Tungsten arc welding and lightweight bonded aluminum honeycomb also were Navaho developments.

Even today the aerodynamic planform of the X-10 and G-26M vehicles is still viewed as modern. Where in the fifties this supersonic Delta/Canard configuration could not be flown by man, today modern digital computer systems allow for a human pilot. Thus, the X-10 and G-26 design has returned in the form of the Euro 2000, the French Rafale and the Swedish Gripen.

No, this is not a history about a long forgotten missile. This is a look into our past, to see where much of our present technology came from. An attempt to show the genesis of our modern aviation and aerospace capability.

Chapter 1
The Beginning

The German Research

Many authors would begin a history of the Navaho project at the issuing of the research contract. The true beginning of the program however is found in the last two years of the second world war. The years when the Germans began firing the worlds first strategic missiles at targets in France and England.

The V-1

As part of the Treaty of Versailles ending the First World War, Germany was forbidden to develop long-range artillery. As a result, after Hitler came to power, in 1937 Germany began developing its rocket technology. By 1942 the Germans were developing the V-1, a pilotless bomber capable of delivering a one ton payload against a target 150 miles away.

By modern standards the V-1 was less than crude. After being catapulted into the air, the vehicle would climb at the angle of its launching ramp until it reached its cruise altitude. During this time, an analog [mechanical] computer would adjust the missile's heading until the V-1's magnetic compass aligned with a preset compass heading. For the rest of the flight the computer would make minor rudder adjustments to keep the missile on this heading.

Once on course and at flight altitude the V-1 would begin gaining speed until it reached approximately 400 mph: at this speed aerodynamic drag equaled engine thrust. Distance

A Navy Loon missile on display at the Chino Air Museum, Calif. The Loon or JB-2 was America's copy of the German V-1. Its primary differences were a radio control system and solid fuel boosters for launch. Otherwise the missiles were the same design and nearly the same performance. Photo by: Author.

flown was determined by the number of rotations a small propeller mounted in the nose made. When this count matched a preset number in the computer, the V-1's elevators were depressed. This caused the missile to pitch downward into the ground.[1]

Though crude by todays standards, in 1943 the V-1 was the most modern weapon in service. At only 25 feet in length, this missile was more difficult to see and track then a manned aircraft. The V-1 also was fast, with a cruise speed of over 400 MPH. Finally, the missile flew at a very low altitude: between 2,000 and 2,500 feet. This added to the difficulty in identifying, tracking and intercepting the V-1. One British defense ministry officer is reported to have stated that it was eight times more difficult to intercept a V-1 than a manned aircraft.

Because of its great speed only the fastest allied interceptors could catch the V-1. The best of these was the British Gloster Meteor jet fighter which could catch the V-1 without modification. Piston engine fighters like the P-51 and the Spitfire however had to be stripped of all armor and even paint to make them as light as possible. They were then fueled with super high octane fuel and had the engine's governors removed. The resulting configuration is seen today in air racers.

Even with these modifications the propeller planes barely could catch the V-1s in level flight. And since the V-1 flew at such a low altitude the planes could not increase their speed by diving because they could not pull out intime to keep from crashing. Eventually the tactic was to have the missile overtake the fighter, which then attacked the V-1 as it passed.

Interesting enough the problem was not catching the V-1, but what to do with it when you did. If a fighter crippled it with a machinegun burst, the V-1's warhead could detonate. Such a detonation [2,000 lbs of TNT] would destroy or cripple any aircraft flying within 150 yards of the missile. British military reports indicate that 37 aircraft were damaged in such explosions with 4 to 5 planes actually being downed. Casualties from these intercepts were 5 pilots and one navigator.

American Counterparts

Now the performance capabilities of the V-1 are very well documented. What is not well documented is how allied missile technology compared to Germany's cruise missile. The first United States service to operate a cruise missile, of sorts, was the U.S. Navy. Called Assault drones, these radio controlled aircraft attacked Japanese targets in the Pacific.

The Assault drone was launched by radio control from either a carrier or a land base. Once airborne, control of the drone was transferred to an airborne aircraft. An operator in this aircraft would then control the drone for the remainder of the flight.

Once in the combat area, the drone controller would guide the vehicle into the target. During the Pacific campaign, several of these drones hit a heavily defended target on Bouganville. Though successful, these drones were model Ts compared to Germany's V-1.

In an initial attempt to correct this technology gap the United States Army Air Force tried to copy the V-1. The weapon they constructed was the JB-2, a V-1 made from parts manufactured by American automotive companies including a Ford pulse jet engine. Though it looked like the V-1, it was not even close in performance. Its engine was inferior, resulting in a lower flight speed. It also used the radio control guidance system used by the assault drones. Though U.S. Army Air Force built many of these missiles for use against Japan, the JB-2s ended their days as air-to-surface test vehicles. Several also were given to the Navy who gave them the name Loon and used them as a test missile for the later Regulus.

An American Assault Drone takes to the air from a U.S. carrier. With fixed landing gear and engines from light observer aircraft these were simple missiles. Originally they were to approach their target ship and launch a torpedo. By the end of the war they simply dove into their target. Photo by: U.S. Navy.

An Assault Drone is prepared for a launch against a Pacific target. Note the early TV camera in the missile's nose. Also note the aerial bomb attached to the missile's center line mount. This was a hold over from the days when the Assault Drones were to bomb their target and return for reuse. Photo by: U.S. Navy.

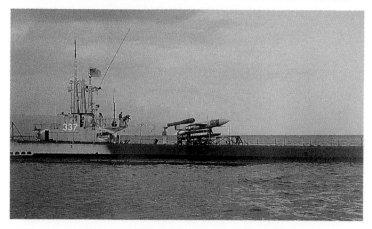

A Navy Loon [SL-115 LTV-N-2 #1046] on the U.S. submarine Carbonerro, 19 May 1949. Experiments with this missile lasted until 1950. By then it was a test bed for the Navy's Regulus Strategic Cruise Missile. Photo by: U.S. Navy.

The V-2

Where the V-1 was more advanced then similar American missiles, the V-2 had no U.S. counterpart. It was a hyper-sonic vehicle in a world of subsonic aircraft: a terror weapon with no equal.

The V-2 had a maximum speed greater than 3,800 MPH (nearly ten times the maximum speed of a P-51 Mustang). No fighter could catch it and no anti-aircraft artillery could target it. On radar sets of the period it was a line not a dot. And since it was outrunning its own sound, the V-2 hit without warning.

The V-2 was the greatest missile the 1940s produced. It could deliver a 2,200 pound payload a distance of 200 miles in less than four minutes. Its guidance was self contained, consisting of two gyroscopes, a mechanical accelerometer, and an analog computer. Finally, the weapon was fully mo-bile, capable of launch from a quickly surveyed launch site.

On the allied side only the American Hermes and GALCIT missile research projects came close to the V-2s technology. The longest range allied rocket was Caltech's Private A, a GALCIT development rocket. It weighed only 350 pounds compared to the V-2s 28,229 and it had a range of only 10 miles. It was unguided, hence a rocket, and it had a payload capacity of 60 pounds. On a military scale it was a long-range bombardment rocket, not a strategic missile.

In all, Germany launched 3,165 V-2s between Septem-ber 8, 1944 and March 27,1945. Regardless of these high numbers, the Germans perfected their weapons too late for them to change the outcome of the war. With the fall of the Third Reich, allied scientists became the inheritors of Germany's extensive research into guided missiles. Piles of engineering and scientific documents, tons of unused mis-siles, and some 600 scientists were quickly shipped to the United States under operation "Paperclip."

The A-9/A-10

As the Paperclip materials arrived in the United States, Ameri-can scientists began to realize just how far German rocket research had progressed. During the debriefings of Werner

A captured German V-2 is raised for launch. The V-2 was a weapon with no equal during the Second World War. After the war the United States extensively tested the weapon at White Sands Missile Range. We also launched one from a carrier deck. Photo by: U.S. Army, White Sands Missile Range.

von Braun and Walter Dornberger[2] numerous papers, design studies, and documents were discovered about then unknown German missiles.

By the end of the war the Germans were developing sur-face-to-air missiles: the Wasserfall, the Enzian, and the Schmetterling. They had launched missiles from bombers: 865 V-1s from Heinkel bombers against England, and a su-personic mini V-2 called the A-5.[3] They had launched rockets from submerged submarines and had developed a wire-guided anti-tank missile. They had even begun production of a wire guided air-to-air missile for use by the ME-262 jet fighter. All this research however was minor compared to the Reich's continued quest for even longer range surface-to-surface missiles.

One such missile was the A-4B, a winged version of the V-2. According to von Braun's research, this missile was to have a range of from 350 to 470 miles. Three test vehicles were flown before January 1945, all being failures. The first two crashed because of guidance problems. The third mis-sile suffered a catastrophic failure of a wing during boost.

A German Wasserfall missile sits on a launch pad while technicians work on it. Actually, its a Hermes A-1 being readied for a launch at White Sands. Like many post war American designs, the Hermes A-1 was a copy of a German missile. Photo by: U.S. Army White Sands Missile Range.

One of the striking aspects of the V-2 was its mobility. Carried on this mobile launch unit, and fired from a portable pad, it was nearly invulnerable to a preemptive strike. The need to match this mobility would be a major reason why many postwar American missiles were small in size and performance. Only when it was realized that a large missile frame was needed to house an atomic warhead did the size and performance of the missiles increase. Photo by: U.S. Army White Sands Missile Range.

Though unsuccessful, these flights laid the technological base for a still longer range missile: the A-9/A-10.

The A-9/A-10 was the world's first viable intercontinental missile design. A monstrous two stage missile consisting of a large A-10 first stage and an A-4B style A-9 second stage. This missile was to have a diameter of 13.5 feet, a length of 112 feet, and a takeoff weight of 188,090 pounds. Its range was estimated to be just over 3,000 miles, but this was enough to reach Moscow or New York from launch sites in central Germany. And as for speed, at 6,500 miles an hour the A-9/A-10 could reach its target in about 30 minutes.

For comparison, the U.S. Titan 1 two stage ICBM was 10 feet in diameter, 98 feet long, and weighed 220,000 pounds – fifteen years later.

In all the German research was massive. They had achieved liquid fuel engine thrusts in the range of 75,000 pounds of thrust. They had developed inertial guidance to a functional level, and developed both radio/radar guidance, and wire guidance technology. Finally, their supersonic aerodynamic data was the best in the world after 3,000+ flights to Mach 3 and altitudes of 100,000 feet.

The only problem American researchers found with the German program was the cost. A whole year's production of potatoes used to make alcohol fuel for the V-2 bombardment. Half the nation's production of electronic devices used in the V-2s guidance systems, or ground support equipment. And if the V-2s cost so much, what would the still larger A-9/A-10 have cost. To have even tried the kind of missile bombardment on New York that England suffered would have destroyed Germany's economy. Thus, the idea of long-range missiles was determined by many researchers to be another symptom of Nazi Germany's madness.

The Russians

Though many U.S. military and government officials wanted to file the Germany research (aka, make it disappear), the post-war world was not what they hoped it would be. The alliance between the United States and the Soviet Union had evaporated as quickly as spilled alcohol fuel. Not only was the USSR developing its own atomic weapons, it dismantled the Peenemunde research facility and shipped the equipment to Russia. There, with the help of captured German scientists, they began using the equipment to make V-2 copies. Called SS-1s in the later NATO code system, these missiles gave the Soviet Union the distinction of having a long-range missile capability in the late 1940s.

To U.S. military planners, Stalin planned to arm these missiles with the nuclear warhead Hitler was unable to develop. With such a warhead he could blast a city with 20,000 tons of TNT while using only one missile. Compared to the alternative of 20,000 missiles each delivering one ton of TNT, the resulting cost reduction changed the V-2 from a high cost terror weapon into a practical military arm.

Surprisingly, the idea of nuclear tipped V-2s was only a minor concern of American military planners. What really concerned American planners was the question, "what if Stalin developed a nuclear tipped A9/A10." It was this question that forced American military leaders into action.

By 1949 the United States was not the only nation launching V-2s. Where we built them out of parts seized from Germany, the Soviet Union actually began making the missiles. Later classified as SS-1s by NATO, they were the first ballistic missile type to become operational after World War Two. Photo by: U.S. Army White Sands Missile Range.

In October of 1945 the Army Air Technical Services Command invited the nation's largest aeronautical corporations to propose a guided missile research project. There were four classes of missiles to be studied: air-to-air, air-to-surface, surface-to-air and surface-to-surface. Ranges varied from 200 miles to 5,000 and payloads were to be at least one ton.

The Post-War Research Projects

The companies that responded to the Army Air Technical Services Command invitation read like a listing of America's major aircraft companies.

There was Bell Aircraft who had recently built the world's first supersonic manned aircraft, the X-1. On April 1, 1946 they received a contract to develop a 100 mile range subsonic missile for launch from Army Air Force B-29 bombers. This project, initially called MX-776, would result in the Rascal air-to-surface missile.

A second manufacturer was Martin Aircraft, the maker of the B-26 Marauder bomber and the large PBY flying boats of the second world war. They proposed a research program

The Bell MX-776 program would develop the Rascal Air-To-Surface missile, shown here being launched from a B-50 bomber. This supersonic weapon was only superior to air-launched V-1s and JB-2s in speed. Otherwise, it was a big, heavy, liquid fuel missile that was difficult to operate. After many years of development it was deployed on the B-47 bomber for a short time. Photo by: U.S. Air Force.

into a 500 mile range pilotless aircraft similar in concept to the V-1. This project, titled MX-771, would result in the Matador ground launched cruise missile.

Consolidated Vultee, the creator of the B-24 liberator bomber and the later intercontinental B-36 Peacemaker bomber also proposed a project. Theirs was a 500 mile range ballistic missile, similar in size to the German V-2. Called MX-774, this project evolved into the famous Atlas Intercontinental Ballistic Missile.

And of course Northrop Aircraft, run by the radical aircraft designer John Northrop also got involved. Their project was a research effort into the feasibility of a 3,000 mile range cruise missile. Called MX-775, this project also exceeded its performance requirement, developing into the Snark intercontinental cruise missile.

Finishing this list was North American Aircraft. The builder of the B-25 bomber and the P-51 fighter, it too had a heritage of producing ground breaking designs. Its proposal, called MX-770, was to research a 500 mile range vehicle with greater accuracy then the V-2. With the issuing of its one year research contract on April 22,1946, the Navaho program was born.

These were only the Army Air Force's strategic missile programs. For a year the GARPA project had been underway to develop an anti-aircraft missile. This project would later produce the BOMARC surface-to-air missile.

The Navy also was developing guided missiles. In 1946 the Navy gave LTV a contract for the Regulus sea-launched strategic nuclear cruise missile. In the air-to-surface category were the Bat and the Kingfisher. In the surface-to-air class there was the Little Joe, the Lark and the Bumblebee projects. And finally, in the air-to-air class was the Gorgon and the Dove.

Even the Army had its programs. In the surface-to-surface category were the Hermes II and the Corporal SRBMs.

A Hermes II missile on its launch pad. The Hermes II tested the potential for large solid fuel ballistic missiles. The large iron wedge in the nose was probably to determine payload capability. Though an all American design internally, it still retains the classic V-2 shape. This same shape also was used by Consolidated Vultee's MX-774 missile and the first Navaho designs. Photo By: U.S. Army White Sands Missile Range.

In the surface-to-air category was the Nike and the Hermes A-1.

MX-770, The Beginning

Before the war ended North American assigned five engineers to begin studying missile technology. Titled the Technology Research Laboratory and hidden behind a door marked "Top Secret," they began studying captured German documents and equipment. The German research of particular interest to NAA involved high thrust engines, inertial guidance, and high speed aerodynamics. By the time the Air Tech-

The Hermes A-1 was one of two surface-to-air missiles designs the United States Army was developing in the late 40's. Though the worst of the German SAM designs, we played with the missile until about 1950. Then the design was dropped in favor of the superior performing Nike Ajax design. Photo By: U.S. Army White Sands Missile Range.

nical Service issued its invitation, they were ready to propose a three stage research effort to study ways of increasing the range of a V-2 size missile.

Part One: A study of the winged V-2 concept von Braun had tried with the A-4B.

Part Two: A study of the feasibility of replacing the V-2s rocket engines with supersonic ramjets (another German development). If the vehicle could be powered by these then the oxidizer (LOX) could be replaced with natural air. The space in the missile allocated for the oxidizer could then be filled with fuel, doubling the range.

Part Three: A study to determine the size and thrust of the rocket booster needed to launch this jet powered, winged, V-2. This was because the ramjets had to be in motion before they could be ignited. Thus, the German A-9/A-10 two stage ballistic missile was redesigned into a cruise missile.

In January of 1947 North American began preliminary design work on the 500 mile range missile. Staff at the Technical Research Laboratory had grown to 43 including twelve PhD.s and eighteen engineers with Masters degrees. Construction of the first NATIV test rocket also was underway.

The NATIV was the first of the Navaho test missiles. A pure research vehicle, it was to test certain key technologies. One of these technologies was a 32 channel FM/FM telemetry system. This system was to transmit data from various sensors built into the missile. This data would then be used to refine the missile's design.

In February of 1947 NAA completed a study of nuclear powered rocket engines: the conclusion was to go with conventional propellants. In March initial studies then began on solid fuel ramjets. Then in April the program took a great stride with the start of development of the KDIA [the Kinetic Double-Integrating Accelerometer].

The KDIA combined the functions of the accelerometer used in the German V-2 and a double integrator unit. This combination unit solved a major problem with auto-navigation systems; the accurate measurement of distance traveled. The first major advance beyond the V-2 guidance system, the KDIA made long-range inertial guidance possible.

About the time NAA developed the KDIA, a serious flaw was discovered in the winged V-2 design. Post war research on the concept had uncovered a severe stability problem.[4] To correct this problem NAA proposed a radically new boost glide missile design. In this new design NAA placed the wing at the rear of the vehicle: an aft wing configuration. Because this new configuration also replaced the rear horizontal fins, NAA added a canard or forward stabilizer to control pitch. This canard design would set the pattern for eight future North American designs.

Soon after North American proposed this new boost glide design, in April of 1947 the Army Air Force dropped the 500 mile range missile. The service then issued a new requirement for a 1,000 mile, 2,500 foot CEP missile capable of carrying a 3,000 pound warhead. Now under these new requirements, in May development began on the XN-1 inertial navigator. The next month the MX-770 program entered Phase II: component development. With funding now at $3.9 million dollars, construction began on a NATIV launch site at Holloman AFB New Mexico.

The NATIV site at Holloman was not the only new construction NAA was undertaking. Back in March, NAA leased a section of the Santa Susanna Mountains from Los Angeles County. With this additional funding construction now began on a special test facility for aerodynamics and rocket engines. Two months later NAA completed its design for a 16"X16" supersonic wind tunnel. Construction of this tunnel then began in October beginning the development of the Santa Susanna facility.

All this new activity caused employment levels at TRL to increase rapidly. By the end of 1947 the MX-770 program had grown to over 500 people. At this new level, North American decided that it was time to turn it into a separate division. Thus, on 1 October 1947 the Technical Research Laboratory became the Aerophysics Laboratory.

The First Spin-off: The F-86 Sabre Jet.
Before the Technical Research Laboratory became the Aerophysics Laboratory, the first technological spin-off occurred from the Navaho program. North American's acquisition of German swept wing research for the project was also seen by NAA's Aircraft Design Group.

During the War, the swept wing ME-163 and ME-262 German fighters were the fastest aircraft to fly in combat. Even the British Gloster Meteor was inferior in speed, even though the Meteor had a superior engine to the ME-262. So obvious was the potential of swept wings that immediately after the war several U.S. Aircraft companies studied the concept.

The ME-262 on display at the Chino Air Museum. The ME-262 revolutionized air combat by showing the potential of jet engines and swept wings. After the war several ME-262s were sent to the United States for evaluation. Surprisingly, most American jets developed immediately after the war were not swept wing. To attain higher speeds more powerful engines were used. Photo by: Author.

Some companies even proposed the development of a swept wing aircraft: Boeing incorporated the design into its initial proposal for the B-47 and the B-52 jet bombers. These designs however tended towards the development of aircraft five to ten years in the future. Few of the companies would develop a swept wing jet aircraft until they had first developed a jet powered aircraft.

NAA's Aircraft Design Group was in a unique position when the swept wing research became available. Unlike the rest of the industry it had a production jet aircraft, the FJ-1 Fury jet. A variant of this design, designated the P-86 was in development for an Air Force interceptor proposal. Very quickly the design group incorporated a swept wing into this new design.

Though initially hesitant on the swept wing concept, the Army Air Force issued a development contract for the new design in 1946. The first prototype flew a year later and im-

The North American FJ-1 during landing on a pitching carrier deck. The FJ-1 became the starting point for the development of the United States first swept wing fighter. From it came both the F-86 Saber jets and the later swept wing Fury jets. Photo by: Rockwell International.

mediately began breaking records for speed and maneuverability. At 680 MPH the fighter was a good 80 miles an hour faster than Lockheed's new twin engine F-80C Shooting Star. This superior speed also held true against Republic's F-84 Thunderjet and McDonnell's F2H banshee. Thus, the P-86, or should I say F-86 Sabrejet, became the top American fighter in 1948.

In addition to the German swept wing data, the F-86 also benefited from the Navaho program's work in electro-mechanical systems. The systems developed to control the NATIV rockets was made available to the NAA Aircraft Design Group. This electro-mechanical technology allowed the Design Group engineers to include a comprehensive powered flight control system in the Sabrejet's design.

The powered flight control system automatically provided compensating forces to the vehicles flight control surfaces. This improved control and thus mobility. Years later when the F-86 faced the swept winged MiG-15 over Korea the powered system gave it a distinct advantage. Add to this a higher level of pilot training and its understandable why the F-86 shot down over 800 enemy aircraft during this conflict.

only accurate to within one mile of its target. This error is due to gyroscopic precession: the building of minor errors in a gyro's rotation over time. As the flight distance increased from 500 to 1,000 miles, so did the flight time and the resulting error.

In the past, the primary method for correcting this problem was to improve the precision of the gyroscopes. The development of these improved gyros however was both difficult and expensive. In a break from tradition, in April of 1948 NAA began studies into a stellar-inertial system. Called the XN-2, this unit was an XN-1 equipped with a daylight star tracker to take regular stellar fixes. The on-board computer would then use this data to correct for precession.

As work began on the new guidance system, on 26 May 1948 NAA launched its first NATIV missile at White Sands. Seven months later the third and last of these test missiles was launched.[6] The most successful of the three it achieved a maximum speed of Mach 2.23 and attained an altitude of 59,000 feet. Though this was less than half the maximum speed of a V-2, and one tenth its maximum altitude, the data gathered was extremely important.

The FJ-2 swept wing fighter in flight. This picture best shows the change in the vehicle's outward appearance. This version of the FJ fighter came many years after the F-86 went into production with the Air Force. The Navy held up production because of reservations over the carrier landing characteristics of the design. Photo by: Rockwell International.

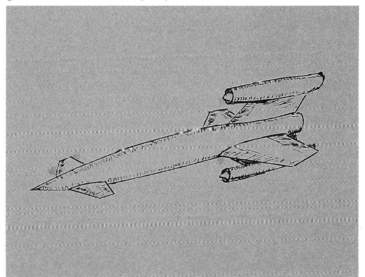

A sketch of the NA-704 design. Some artist renderings were made of this missile design by a Mr. Dusty Carter. Unfortunately, like many Navaho related material, this author was not able to get a copy of one of these rare prints. The best available was this sketch. Photo by: Author.

Aerophysics Laboratory
Now a new division, Aerophysics began 1948 by releasing a preliminary design for the 1,000 mile range missile. Called the XSSM-A-2[5] by the Army Air Force, this missile was the final phase of the original MX-770 proposal. Launched by an integral rocket booster, this missile then cruised to its target under the power of two ramjet engines. Guidance was to be inertial [not radio controlled] and the missile was to dive on its target.

Because of its increased range, in April NAA concluded that the missile needed an enhanced guidance unit. After 30 minutes of flight, the in development XN-1 inertial unit was

During the NATIV flights several important events occurred. In June the Electro-Mechanical Division completed the design of the XN-1. Then in July, the Aerophysics Laboratory moved from the Los Angeles to an old Consolidated Vultee plant in Downey, California. There it would share quarters with NAA's Electro-Mechanical Division.

Two months after the move, preliminary design began of the XN-2 star-tracker INU. Then, in October NAA completed construction of the 16 x 16 inch Mach 3.5 wind tunnel at Santa Susanna. Thus, the year 1948 ended on a high note for North American. Unfortunately, the end of 1948 meant the start of something else for the rest of the world.

The Cold War Begins

As North American progressed towards the development of a 1,000 mile range missile, tensions between the United States and the Soviet Union were rising. The Soviet Union's support for the creation of communist governments in China, Greece and the nations of eastern Europe had made it an enemy. Then, in June of 1948 Soviet troops began a land blockade of Berlin.

The Soviets hoped to get western troops to leave the city without a fight. Thanks to American transport aircraft however the city held out for eleven months. Then, realizing that the plan was not working, Stalin ordered the siege lifted on 19 May 1949. By then he had another way to pressure the west.

Just three months after the Berlin crisis ended, on 29 August the Soviet Union detonated its first atomic bomb. Over night the tensions between the two nations rose to stratospheric levels. Not only was the United States monopoly on nuclear weapons over, but Stalin had the missiles to carry the warhead. Now more than ever the United States government and military had to know if long-range nuclear missiles were possible.

An Army crew loading a 280mm may seem a little out of place in a book on a missile program, but it serves a purpose. Immediately after the Soviets detonated their atomic bomb the U.S. began scrounging for nuclear delivery systems. As a result, the Army rebored this gun from 240mm to 280mm so it could fire a nuclear round. This is an example of the lengths the government was willing to go in order to be able to deploy tactical nuclear warheads. Photo By: U.S. Army.

An early Corporal missile sits on a launch pad at White Sands. Part of the wartime Galcit program, this missile was a development test vehicle for a larger weapon called the Colonel. The Soviet bomb changed that, and in December of 1949 Congress approved of the nuclear arming of the Corporal. A few years later Army units began training with this crude missile. Its radio command system was unreliable and its red fuming nitric acid fuel was both toxic and corrosive. Photo By: U.S. Army, White Sands.

A Navy Regulus sits on a catapult trolley during early Navy tests. The Regulus was so similar in performance to the proposed Martin Matador that in 1949 the Air Force was required to use the Navy missile. This was a cost saving action, nothing more. Within a few months of the Soviet bomb blast however, both programs received a new emphasis and additional funding. Photo By: LTV.

Before this event, federal budget cuts had caused many of the MX-700 series projects to languish. Programs like North Americans MX-770 and Bells MX-776 were developing weapons, but the designs were limited in scope and budget. Other MX-700 series programs had been canceled, including Consolidated Vultee's MX-774 in June of 1947. As the bomb detonated, the Air Force was canceling Martin's MX-771 ground launched cruise missile. Replacing it was a ground launched version of the Navy's Regulus missile. These actions were all based on an Intelligence community conclusion that the Soviet Union would not produce a bomb before 1951.

Adding to the rise in tensions was the fall of Nationalist China in September. With Chinese communists in complete control of mainland China, the communist world had more than doubled. And Stalin was the absolute leader of the communist world.

With the Soviets ahead of schedule on building a bomb and China going communist the United States began reviving its missile programs. The Air Force rescinded the MX-771's cancellation, allowing testing of XB-61 Matador missiles to begin at White Sands. Additional funding was also made available to Bell's RASCAL and Northrop's Snark programs. Congress even gave the Army permission to equip the Corporal missile with a nuclear warhead.

XSSM-A-2 And Further

While all this was going on, North American moved closer to the development of a 1,000 mile range missile. In June 1949 the Electro-Mechanical division completed the detailed design of the XN-1, and in September NAA aerodynamcists fixed the aerodynamic design of the XSSM-A-2. Then, as the year ended, in November the propulsion group tested a 3,000 pound thrust [uncooled] version of the XSSM-A-2's booster engine. A month later Wright Aeronautical completed the major design work on the ramjets. That same month the Electromechanical also completed its prototype XN-1 guidance unit. Two months later all work on XSSM-A-2 ceased.

By the winter of 1949 three XSSM-A-2 airframes were in production. No information is available as to why it was suddenly canceled, but it can be assumed the changing world situation was a factor. Rapid advances in technology also contributed to the demise of this design.

While development of the XSSM-A-2 was underway, back in mid-1948 North American began a study into a 5,000 mile range missile. Except for the range, the specifications were the same as the XSSM-A-2. The new design also was to use the XSSM-A-2's ramjets, rocket engine, and inertial guidance unit.

To achieve a 5,000 mile range missile under these parameters North American designers began work on a two stage vehicle. By switching from an internal to an external rocket booster, NAA engineers could improve vehicle range in several ways. First, because the rocket engine was only used in launch, by removing it the missile would be lighter during cruise flight. Second, by removing the engine more space became available for jet fuel. Finally, by mounting the booster systems externally NAA could increase the number of engines used and the capacity of the fuel tanks. The result was a more powerful booster that could carry the missile to a higher altitude. At altitudes of over 70,000 feet the vehicle

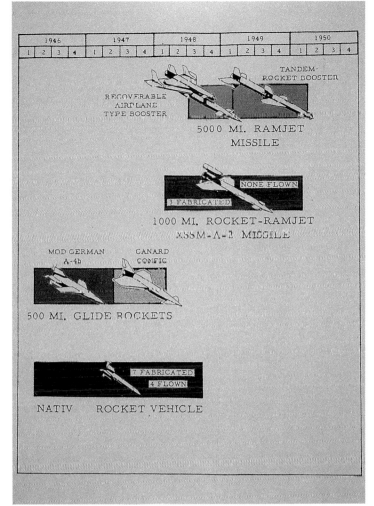

This chart shows the different vehicles produced or designed in the first five years of the MX-770 program. The chart also gives a general idea of when the work on these designs began and when they ended. The chart goes from bottom up showing first the NATIV and booster glide missile designs. In the middle is the NA704 design or XSSM-A-2 missile. Finally at the top are the two long range designs developed during prior to the start of WS-104A. Photo by: Author.

could fly more efficiently, extending range.

The initial combination of these changes was an extraordinary design that was years ahead of its time. The flight missile was a medium sized ramjet powered drone of the delta canard style. Carrying it piggy back was its winged, recoverable booster unit. Today, this design could be mistaken for a suborbital scramjet powered aircraft.

In early 1949 North American dropped the recoverable booster for a disposable sequential stage design. This missile design looks like an extra large Talos surface-to-air missile, then in development for the Navy. Work on this design continued into the first quarter of 1950 when NAA canceled it too. Replacing it would be the most ambitious design of all, a 5,500 mile range missile capable of carrying a 7,000 pound payload. This marks the beginnings of the XSM-64 phase of the Navaho program.

The Second Spin-off

On 25 June 1950 the North Korean Army invaded South Korea. The start of this war resulted in a massive increase in

Shades of the first long range Navaho design, a Lockheed A-12 carries a D-21 ramjet drone between its twin tails. This concept for both extending reconnaissance range and speed over target was tried several times. One has to wonder if Lockheed engineers knew of the 1948 North American design when they came up with this combination. Photo By: Lockheed Aircraft.

U.S. military spending. All the surviving missile programs were accelerated: the Air Force even resurrected Consolidated's [now Convair's] MX-774 missile.

One of these projects was the Army's Hermes C-1 program. The Hermes program had undergone many changes since its beginnings in the Second World War, testing different types of ballistic missiles. Hermes C-1 was a project to develop a 500 mile range ballistic missile. Begun in June of 1946, it had remained a research program as a result of post war funding cuts.

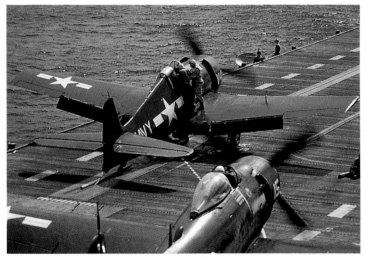

Regardless of all the missile research begun after World War II, when the Korean war began the United States was no better off. Here we see a Hellcat drone being prepared for launch from the USS Boxer, September 1952. An updated version of the Assault Drones, this missile was used against targets in Korea. Seen in this picture is the AD-1 mother ship which controlled the drone. Photo by: U.S. Navy.

The start of the Korean War revitalized the Hermes C-1 program. On 11 September 1950 the Army moved the program from Fort Bliss Arkansas to Redstone Arsenal Alabama. Soon after this the missile's maximum payload weight was increased to that of a Mk-6 nuclear warhead: cutting the range to 200 miles.

While all this was going on, in October of 1950 NAA tested the XSSM-A-2 engine to its full rated thrust of 75,000 pounds. This was the first all American made engine to achieve the thrust of the German engines. The new engine also operated for 57 seconds and produced a specific impulse of 215 pounds of thrust for every pound-per-second of fuel flow. Almost immediately it became the selected engine for the new Army missile. Two years later, on 8 April 1952 the Hermes C program was given a new name: Redstone.

The selection of the original Navaho engine for the Redstone would make this engine more famous then the pro-

The Hellcat succeeds in getting off the deck. While these drones were hitting targets at 350 miles per hour, Loons were flying at 500. The Navy also was flying Regulus cruise missiles and the Air Force was testing Matadors. Photo by: U.S. Navy.

gram that developed it. Over the next decade this engine would launch nuclear warheads, send America's first satellite into orbit, and then orbit our nation's first astronauts.

Weapon System 104-A

One month after the Korean War began, in July of 1950 the Air Force officially issued North American new performance requirements for the Navaho missile. These new requirements called for intercontinental range (5,500 nautical miles), a flight speed of no less than Mach 3, and a flight altitude greater than 60,000 feet. The missile also was to carry 7,000 pounds of payload and have a CEP of 1,500 feet. In accordance with these new requirements the program was given a new name: Weapon System 104-A.

tem for the final Navaho missile. It also would extend the aerodynamic, structure and guidance tests to speeds of Mach 2.75 and distances of 1,500 miles.

Phase Three would then see the creation of the G-38 missile. The prototype for the Navaho missile system, it would be the last test missile before deployment.

As part of the program changes, in the summer of 1950 Sandia National Laboratory officials met with North American. The purpose of this meeting was to determine what nuclear device the Navaho would carry. At that time North American planned a payload area capable of handling a device 60 inches in diameter and 90 inches long. This was exactly the dimensions of a 20 kiloton W-4 warhead [an advanced Fat Man bomb]. From that time forward Navaho was to be a nuclear weapon.

So ended the beginning of the Navaho program. Though it started as a 500 mile range winged V-2, it had evolved into an Intercontinental nuclear weapon. Now comes the history of the development of this missile. A history of technological successes in the X-10, and engineering frustrations with the G-26. It is also a history of a development and testing program whose advances would forever change the face of American aerospace.

NOTES

(1) This sharp dive made the fuel in the V-1's fuel tanks slosh forward. This starved the missile's pulse jet engine causing a pre-impact engine shutdown. The sudden silence turned into a warning for Londoners to duck for cover.

(2) Walter Dornberger was the commander of the Peene-munde research facility.

(3) The A5 was a supersonic test vehicle for the V-2. Though not deployed as a weapon system, it had significant potential.

(4) Though not specified, the problem probably centered on the vehicle's center of gravity moving back to the tail during flight. As the fuel was burned, the vehicle's weight would concentrate in the engine section. The CG thus moved aft while the vehicle's center of lift [due to the wings] stayed in the center. This made the winged V-2 highly unstable.

(5) North American designated this design NA-704.

(6) An unconfirmed report states North American flew four NATIV missiles. This source also states NAA made seven NATIVs at its El Segundo facility.

A Redstone during launch. The selection of the Navaho engine for this missile was based on one criteria: availability. The Redstone had to be operational in the shortest possible time to counter potential Soviet nuclear aggression. Years later the selection of this engine would help to make this missile famous. Photo by: U.S. Army, Redstone Arsenal.

Because of the new performance requirements, North America proposed a three phase program for WS-104-A.

Phase One involved the construction and testing of the X-10 drone missile. This vehicle would test the aerodynamics, structure, autopilot and the inertial navigator of the Navaho missile up to a speed of Mach 2.

Phase Two involved the creation and testing of the G-26 drone missile. This vehicle would test the vertical launch sys-

Chapter 2
Weapon System 104A Phase One

The X-10

The X-10 is by all standards the most famous of the Navaho vehicles. The only missile to be classified as an X-plane, it appears from time-to-time in books and videos. It also was the most successful of the Navaho missiles, completing over 20 flights.

Preliminary design of the X-10 began in May of 1950. The first wind tunnel tests at Santa Susanna began in December and in February 1951 North American completed the preliminary design. The next month the design was successfully tunnel tested up to Mach 2.87. Three months later, in June the United States Air Force Bombardment Aircraft and Guided Missile Board inspected the mockup.

SPECIFICATIONS (X-10)

Dimensions

Length: 66' 2"	Height: 14' 5"
Span: 28' 2"	Wing Area:425 sq. feet

Weight: Maximum Takeoff - 42,300 pounds
Design Takeoff - 35,000 lbs.
Empty - 25,800 lbs.

Performance
Speed: Maximum - Mach 2.08 Range: 818 miles
Altitude: Maximum - 50,000'

Propulsion
Two Westinghouse XJ40-WE-1 turbojet engines with afterburners.
Thrust: Afterburner - 10,900 lbs. each for 60 minutes
Military - 7,250 lbs. each for 60 minutes
Continuous - 6,500 lbs. each

Guidance

Airborne Radio Command:	Receiver - AN/ARW-56
	Decoder - Bell Model 109
Ground Control Station:	Transmitter - AN/ARW-55
Radar Tracking: Transponder -	AN/APW-11A
Ground Station -	AN/MSQ-1
Vehicle Control:	Autopilot - PIX10
	Telemetering -

Payload: 7,000 lbs. of instrumentation
Number Manufactured: 13

The X-10 mockup was more than impressive, it was futuristic. The X-10 was the first aircraft of the low wing delta/canard configuration. Dimensionally the missile was twice as long and almost twice as high as North American's earlier P-51 Mustang fighter. Yet regardless of its size, every bit of space was used.

Starting from the front was the nose compartment. Here was housed the radio command and telemetering antennas needed for flight control and some ballast. Behind the nose [from the very front of the canard to its trailing edge] was the guidance compartment. Inside here would be the autonavigator when it was selected. Because the XN-2 used a star tracker a circular window was located on the top of the section. This compartment was air-conditioned and pressurized.

This drawing of the X-10 is used quite often to describe the missile's layout. This picture shows the general structure, position of various components, etc. Its an excellent engineer style drawing, though you may have to be an engineer to fully appreciate it. Photo by: William F. Gibson Jr.

Another drawing of the X-10 layout. This exploded view drawing is not accurate, but it is easier to see the different component sections of the missile. Photo by: Joe Pomykata.

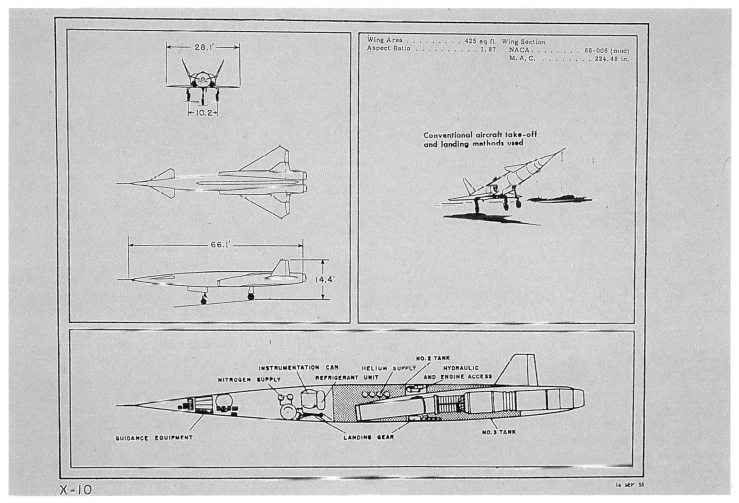

Wing Area . . . . 425 sq ft   Wing Section
Aspect Ratio . . . . 1.87   NACA . . . . 66-006 (mod)
                                    M. A. C. . . . . 224. 46 in.

Conventional aircraft take-off
and landing methods used

INSTRUMENTATION CAN   HELIUM SUPPLY   NO. 2 TANK   HYDRAULIC
NITROGEN SUPPLY   REFRIGERANT UNIT   AND ENGINE ACCESS

GUIDANCE EQUIPMENT   LANDING GEAR   NO. 3 TANK

X-10   14 SEP 55

These drawings come from an Air Force Missile Characteristics document. They show the vehicle in three views and a general internal layout. The combination of these three views gives you all the information you need to fully visualize this missile. Photo by: U.S. Air Force.

Behind the guidance compartment was the forward fuel tank [approximately 565 gallons]. Though needed for the final design, on the X-10 this was a false tank used to house radio command equipment. After the forward fuel tank came the warhead compartment [another false title]. Here was located the PIX10 autopilot, the telemetry system transmitters, the cooling system and the nose gear. All of these would not be needed on the operational missile.

After the warhead section was the main fuel tank which carried 2,100 gallons of jet fuel. Also contained in the fuel tank were the fuel pumps, helium pressurization bottles and several tubes. These tubes carried heated hydraulic oil from the X-10's heat exchangers to the fuel tank. Thus, the main fuel tank was also a large heat sink for the vehicle's air conditioning system.

Behind the main tank was the engine accessory section. This section housed the hydraulic pumps for the landing gear and the flight control systems. The compartment also housed the number three and four fuel tanks. Of these two tanks, only number three [710 gallons] was ever used during the program. Number four carried over 200 gallons of ballast fuel and the parachute. All tanks were pressurized to 4.5 PSI with a limit of 6.5 PSI.

Propulsion for the X-10 came from two XJ40 afterburning turbojet engines. These engines were the most powerful turbine engines available when the program began. The J40 also was a troublesome engine with few aircraft ever flying under its power. Each engine had a Sundstrand 30 KVA alternator to produce electrical power. Only one of these alternators was needed for a flight.

All these factors combined to produce an aircraft that weighed as much empty as a fully loaded F-104, F-100 or F-102 fighter. Only the F-101 Voodoo and the F-105 Thunderchief equaled the X-10 in weight: empty and maximum take-off. More importantly, none of the designs could match the X-10's speed.

Performance

If the dimensions of the vehicle were impressive, so was the performance. The X-10 was one of the first jet aircraft to have a thrust-to-weight ratio greater than one half [0.51]. Where North American's three year old F-86 Sabrejet could just reach Mach 1 in a dive, the X-10 could cruise at Mach 2. On a typical test mission, without afterburner, the X-10 could climb to 35,000 feet in 6.7 minutes. By comparison Lockheed's F-80 Shooting Star could just reach 25,000 feet in seven minutes. And at full afterburner, the X-10 could climb at over 20,000 feet-per-minute: almost twice the climb rate of the F-86. All factors considered, the X-10 was superior to any fighter in service in 1951.

Of course to compare the X-10 to any manned aircraft is improper. The manned fighters are inherently heavier than

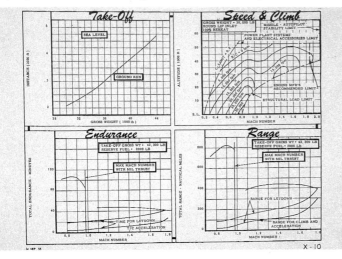

This picture is of a performance table taken from the Air Force Missile Characteristics document. Shown is the X-10s performance during Takeoff, Speed & Climb, Endurance and Range under specific conditions. Photo by: U.S. Air Force.

cruise missiles because they are designed for high G maneuvers. Manned fighters also had to survive 1.5 times their expected maximum aerodynamic loading.[2] The X-10s however only had to sustain 1.25 times their expected maximum aerodynamic loading: significantly lower than the fighters. These two design differences meant that the X-10 always had a superior thrust-to-weight ratio over manned fighters with similar engine thrusts.

Surprisingly, when compared to aircraft with superior thrust-to-weight [TOW] ratios, the X-10 still had superior performance. The F-102 Delta Dagger, a delta wing fighter first flown in 1954, had a TOW of 0.61. Yet when in flight it could barely exceed Mach 1.25. The F-104 Starfighter had a TOW of 0.55 but it topped out at Mach 1.9. Neither aircraft could have caught the X-10 in flight and both had either limited range, payload, or altitude compared to this test vehicle.

X-10 Versus the F-102
The X-10 design had several superior features to that of the F-102 Delta Dagger. At subsonic speeds the X-10 had less parasite drag due to its smaller wing area [425 sq. ft. to 695 sq. ft.]. This smaller wing was possible because the X-10's canard allowed a higher takeoff angle of attack. On the tailless delta F-102, its angle of attack at low speeds was far smaller reducing the lifting capability of the wing. This in turn meant a larger wing had to be used, increasing the aerodynamic drag.

At transonic speed the F-102 was officially superior due to its area rule body. The term "officially" is used because the

X-10 was not an area rule aircraft. The X-10's canard/delta design however made for a more gradual drag build up than would occur in a regular wing tail design. Thus, the drag differences at transonic speed were minor.

At speeds beyond Mach 1 however, the X-10 had a higher fineness ratio then the F-102 [length/frontal area]. This meant

A YF-102A Delta dagger fighter in flight. At this angle, this manned contemporary of the X-10 looks practically rotund. It was supposed to have Mach 2 capabilities, long range, and high maneuverability. In testing and in service however, it was just barely able to exceed Mach 1 and had limited range. Poor engine ducts [particularly on this prototype], a large body and limited engine thrust kept performance down. Photo by: U.S. Air Force, Edwards AFB.

that the X-10 had less supersonic wave drag, a major form of drag above Mach 1. This reduced wave drag when added to the vehicle's lower parasite drag made the X-10 the sleeker of the two aircraft. Thus, at altitude and full power, the X-10 could out run the higher powered F-102.

The X-10 Versus The F-104
Where the F-102 had a lower fineness ratio than the X-10, the opposite was true with the F-104. In this comparison the F-104's problem is a wing leading edge sweep of only 40 degrees. This low sweep angle means that the F-104 always has a supersonic leading edge at speeds above Mach 1.25. This meant that the F-104's aerodynamic drag increased significantly after reaching this Mach number.

The X-10 leading edge sweep however was 60 degrees. This gave the missile a subsonic leading edge at speeds up to Mach 2. Thus its aerodynamic drag was significantly lower then the F-104's between Mach numbers 1.25 and two.

Adding to this drag problem, the F-104 Starfighter also had no area rule. This made the drag buildup at Mach one extremely high. The X-10's design was thus more efficient, allowing Mach two flight with lower thrust engines.

Intake Ducts
No discussion of the superiority of the X-10 to contemporary fighters can be complete without mentioning the X-10's engine ducts.

The X-10 is the first jet vehicle to have a converging/diverging inlet duct for its engines. Before the X-10, U.S. fighter

An F-104 Starfighter during a William tell bombing competition. The F-104 was another contemporary design to the X-10. It too was to have Mach 2 speed and reasonable range. Unlike the heavier F-102, the F-104 was a lightweight fighter designed for aerial combat. Regardless of this It took years to fully develop and had only limited U.S. service. Photo by: U.S. Air Force.

designers used normal shock engine ducts in their designs. Both the prototype YF-100, YF-102 and YF-104 aircraft used normal shock intake ducts.

In a normal shock duct, a strong supersonic shock occurs at the duct entrance. Across this shock air speed drops below Mach 1. This is a desirable quality because if supersonic air hits a turbine blade, the blade will break. Air pressure, temperature and air density are also increased across this shock. This improves engine efficiency since it takes less power to compress the air for combustion.

The problem with normal shock ducts is that they are the

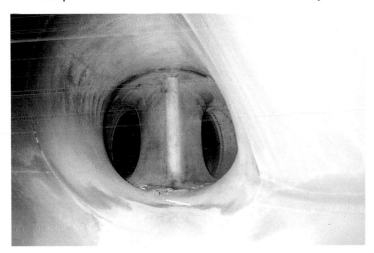

Looking down the engine intake of the X-10 at Wright Patterson AFB. Here we can just see the converging [narrowing] and then diverging [widening] aspect of these ducts. Though more efficient then a spiked inlet, these ducts were more difficult to design. These ducts also were fixed, limiting their maximum effectiveness to a narrow speed range. At any other speed [higher or lower] their effectiveness diminishes. Photo by: Author.

least efficient of the three duct types available. The most efficient is the converging/diverging duct system used by the X-10. In this design the first shock is an oblique shock deep inside the duct. Across this shock pressure, temperature and air density increase like in a normal shock. The difference is however that the air speed does not drop below Mach 1.

In the X-10 style of duct multiple oblique shocks occur gradually reducing the air speed while building pressure, temperature, and air density. When the duct splits, a weak normal shock then occurs bringing the air speed below Mach 1. The result is the highest possible pressure, temperature and air density entering the jet engine's compressor stage.

The problem with the converging/diverging design in the 1950s was its complexity. A simpler design is a spiked diffuser that produces an initial oblique shock before the air flow entered the duct. Then, at the ducts entrance, a weaker normal shock occurred. When the ducts of the F-104, F-102, and F-105 fighters were redesigned, variations of this concept were used. The production F-104s used a standard spike, visible in photos of this aircraft. The F-102 had a ledge added to the duct on the body side [this ledge produced an oblique shock]. The F-105 was the strangest of all with its reverse slope ducts.

One final note on the X-10's intake ducts: the vehicle had a passive laminar bleed system. In this system turbulent boundary layer air flows into a group of ducts between the main intake duct and the vehicle body. This system reduced air turbulence in the air entering the main duct, improving efficiency further.

None of the early supersonic jets had such a system. In later military aircraft like the F-4 phantom a passive system is used. In this system the intake ducts are moved out from the side of the aircraft. Between the intakes and the vehicle body

A front, port quarter, view of the YF-104 prototype. Here we see the early style, normal shock engine intakes. These limited the effectiveness of the F-104's engine and reduced maximum speed. The aircraft's performance was further inhibited by its low thrust engine and limited leading edge sweep. Photo by: Lockheed Aircraft.

A side view of a F-104A Starfighter. Here we see the spiked inlet used on the production aircraft. Many fighters of this period had major changes made to their intakes after the fabrication of prototypes. The F-104, the F-102, and the F-105 are just a few examples. Photo by: U.S. Air Force.

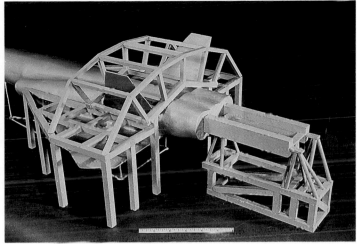

A wooden model of the horizontal test fixture used to static test the X-10. Outside of descriptions by North American engineers, this is all we have to describe the facility. The "I" beams are depicted by two wooden blocks. The fixture rested over the X-10's rudders and wings. Photo by: William F. Gibson Jr.

is a smooth channel. This channel allows the near body turbulent air to move past without creating excessive aerodynamic drag.

Construction and Testing

With the inspection board's approval, in September of 1951 North American released the detailed design for the X-10.

The entrance to the X-10's engine intake. Here we see the laminar bleed ducts just between the missile body and intake. 90 percent of the air taken in by these ducts was expelled to the atmosphere from vents on the top and bottom of the duct. The remaining ten percent of the air was used to purge the engine compartment of vapors. On modern fighters the engine inlets are moved out from the body and a channel is created to allow the turbulent air to pass. Though effective, it does nothing to cleanse the engine compartment of fuel vapors. Photo by: Author.

Fabrication of the first X-10 [No. Three, GM-19309] was completed at North American's Downey division in December of 1952. Soon after this NAA engineers placed the missile in a special test apparatus called the "Horizontal Test Facility." To simulate lift loads, several hundred bicycle spokes were connected to the wings of the X-10. These spokes were in turn

connected to whiffle trees. The sequence in which the spokes were grouped on the whiffle trees dictated the type of loading being simulated.

To produce engine thrust loads, two large "I" beams were inserted into the X-10's empty engine nacelles and mounted to the supports. These beams were moved up and down [in tandem or together] to force the vehicle's body to move in specific directions. This movement was restrained by the whiffle trees, producing strain on the bicycle spokes. According to the vehicle's design, the bicycle spokes would break before any structure components.

An interesting problem in static testing the X-10 was the simulation of aerodynamic heating [heating from air friction] on the vehicle. Since the X-10 was to fly at speeds over Mach 2, air friction could produce surface temperatures of up to 470 degrees Fahrenheit. At this temperature stainless steel looses a tenth of its structural strength. To simulate at room temperature, the static load on the vehicle body had to be increased by over 12%.

Where the X-10s stainless steel (18-8) body lost 10% of its strength at 470 degrees, the vehicle's aluminum wings lost 50%. Thus, to simulate the strain, the static loading on the wings had to be twice that expected. North American engineers had to make sure that they did not over stress the missile's steel body while they stressed the aluminum wings to the required loading.

No ultimate level tests were performed, only limit load tests. These static tests were completed in early 1953 following which the airframe was sent back to the assembly line for completion. Then, in May of 1953 the first flight ready X-10 was trucked to Edwards AFB.

The X-10 Flight Test Program, Edwards AFB

Before the first X-10 arrived at Edwards AFB, three special aircraft arrived to begin the testing program. The first of these planes was an F-86D equipped with the prototype PIX10

autopilot. Its role was to prove this autopilot before the first X-10 flight test. It also had modified dive brakes to simulate those of the X-10. Testing of this aircraft began in the December of 1952.

The second aircraft was a QF-80 drone aircraft. This aircraft was equipped with the X-10's radio control system. Its primary mission was to simulate the X-10 for the training of the ground control pilots. This included initial testing of the automatic approach and landing system. Flights with this aircraft also began in December of 1952.

The final aircraft was the ET-33 flight control aircraft. This aircraft carried an airborne control unit, allowing it to control the X-10 during takeoff, cruise flight and landings. Nearly all of the X-10 takeoffs from Edwards were under the control of this aircraft.

North American trucked the first X-10 [GM19307] to Edwards AFB in May of 1953. On arrival the Air Force brought a crane over to move it from the truck down to the ground.

During this operation however, the crane's clutch slipped dropping the vehicle back down on the truck bed. On impact the main wheels became wedged into the wheel chucks embedded in the truck bed. To free the vehicle almost required tearing apart the truck bed. Damage to the main gear was minor however and North American did not have to return the vehicle to the Downey facility.

Functional ground tests of the X-10 began at Edwards in June of 1953. During these tests the Air Force subjected the vehicle to radio noise to see if it interfered with any of the vehicle's electro-mechanical systems. Then number one's airframe and engine cooling system were tested. Finally, the Air Force subjected the vehicle to a combined systems test, completing the ground test program.

Taxi Tests
No.1
With static ground testing completed, on 3 September 1953

Left: A P-80 Shooting Star in flight. When the MX-770 program began the P-80 was the top of the line in U.S. fighters. By the time the first X-10s were being built it was completely obsolete. Many were converted into radio controlled target drones to test new missile systems. One of these drones was loaned to North American Aviation to help test the X-10's radio control and closed loop landing systems. Photo By: U.S. Air Force, Edwards AFB.

Opposite: A side view of GM19307 [X-10 number one] on the lake bed at Edwards AFB. Note the vertical radio antenna just behind the canards. During the initial flights, this antenna received command inputs from the ET-33 or ground controllers. During the supersonic flights however an internal antenna was used. Photo by: Rockwell International.

the first taxi test occurred. This operation was to test the vehicle's ground steering and stopping characteristics in a simulated landing. Missile control was by the ET-33 which rolled along side and 300 feet to the left of the missile.

The test count down began at 4:00 AM Pacific time. Minor problems caused several delays ranging in duration from 15 to 45 minutes. Then at 4:06 PM the X-10's engines were set to military RPM and the chocks were released.

Now free to move the X-10 quickly accelerated to 50 knots. At this speed a full left heading command was issued [and obeyed]. Then the ET-33 issued a full right command bringing the missile back onto its original heading. This test

The missile then came to a full stop in 0.43 miles. This made a total taxi run of 2.6 miles.

No.2

The second [high speed] taxi test was originally planned for 21 September 1953. Problems with an inverter on the Sundstrand alternator occured producing an irregular voltage in the vehicle. The countdown was thus halted for repairs.

A second attempt was made on 22 September. Minor holds caused some delays but the countdown continued to X minus 5 seconds. Then vibrations caused by the engines being brought to full afterburner caused the parachute door to open. The chute opened in the afterburner exhaust and promptly caught fire. The taxi test was immediately canceled.

With a new parachute, countdown began again on 24 September 1953. Shortly after engine start however, a malfunction occurred in the right rudder and elevon control. Dur-

This picture shows X-10 number one and the ET-33 control aircraft roaring down the lake bed. This may be a picture of the first taxi test in which both vehicles rolled down the lake bed together. An argument for this is the lack of stripping on the X-10. This would indicate the early vehicle color scheme. Photo by: U.S. Air Force, Edwards AFB.

completed the missile was then accelerated again up to 80 knots.

The simulated touchdown command was issued approximately 2.17 miles from the missile's starting point. The engines went to idle RPM and the parachute was deployed.

ing shutdown the voltage regulators were turned off before the engines stopped. This caused a high voltage spike on the 28 volt electrical bus to the F-45 inverter. Noting an increase in inverter output, engineers disconnected the unit from the system. This action cut all power to the engine throttle

X-10 number one sits with its parachute out behind it. The vehicle is at a dead stop but the chute is in full blossom. The parabrake was a constant source of problems to the X-10s at Edwards. Most of the landings occurred with this unit failing to operate properly. Photo by: Rockwell International.

servo allowing the throttle to move to the full afterburner position. Fuel then dumped into the engine exhaust causing a small fire. No damage was done to the X-10, but the incident was extremely notable.

After cleaning up and checking out 19307, at midnight of 29 September 1953 North American again began a countdown for the high speed taxi test. Two long holds were implemented in order to make throttle adjustments and to replace a leaking valve on the air conditioning system. Then at 15:40 PST the engines were set to full afterburner and the chocks were released.

Under the control of the airborne ET-33, X-10 number 1 roared forward. As speed increased so did the vehicle's pitch angle until the nose wheel was fully extended. At 2,800 feet down the runway it had reached 135 knots or 155 MPH. For the next 2,400 feet the missile held this speed; its nose wheel sometimes coming off the ground. Then the simulated touchdown began with the parachute deploying 3,000 feet later.

1.2 miles after the TD simulation began the differential brakes were applied. The missile then came to a halt 1,400 feet later. The total distance traveled was 2.5 miles.

Minor problems occurred with the telemetry system, otherwise the test was successful. X-10 number one was now ready for its first flight.

Flight Testing
Flight testing the X-10 was a complex operation involving many people and vehicles. In the first flights, the ET-33 aircraft controlled the takeoff and landing of the X-10. Later, as the program progressed, the X-10 used the automatic approach and landing system for recovery. As for vehicle control during cruise flight, the purpose of the flight dictated the equipment used. If the vehicle was making a speed run, the X-10 was radio controlled from the ground. Tracking was by radar with some visual information provided by an F-100 chase aircraft. If it was a subsonic test, control could be from the ground or the ET-33.

One of the interesting features of the X-10's automatic landing system was a device called the Lateral Optical Tracker [LOT]. More commonly called the Hero Scope, this device was a surveyors transit connected to a radio control transmitter. Placed at the far end of the runway, and aligned with the center line, this device controlled the vehicle during final approach and landing.

During approach the X-10 was tracked by SCR-554 radar units. As the vehicle approaches zero elevation, these radars lose their ranging accuracy. At this point the missile's descent rate and flare point were set on automatic. Lateral control was then turned over to the hero scope operator [hero pilot].

The hero pilot would sight the X-10 when the vehicle was about 1,500 feet off the runway. He would then rotate the LOT as needed to see the vehicle through the scope. Any movement of the scope away from the center line would produce a radio signal. The X-10s guidance system would detect this signal and adjust the rudders to bring the vehicle back to the centerline. Once aligned with the runway centerline

the signal would stop and the rudders would go to neutral.

By keeping the X-10 in the scope's cross hair's during approach, the "Hero Pilot" kept the missile from drifting out of the runway approach route. At a specific altitude, determined by the X-10's radar altimeter, the vehicle would then flare insuring that the main gears touched ground first. The nose wheel would then be automatically lowered and the X-10 would begin its landing roll.

After touchdown, the Lateral Optical Tracker's would continue to follow the vehicle down the runway until it stopped. As during approach, if the vehicle drifted off the centerline the operator would turn the tracker to follow it. This movement would then send an adjustment signal to the X-10's guidance system. This time however, the guidance system would vary the strength of the X-10s brakes to produce the required correction.

North American engineers bestowed the name Hero Scope for this device so the operator could be called the Hero Scope operator. This is a fitting title for this gentleman who stood and watched a 20,000 pound vehicle come at him at potentially 160 knots. One should particularly note that if the parabrake did not open this 20,000 pound vehicle could run him down after it ran off the runway.

Surprisingly the scope operator was not in any real danger. If an X-10 over ran the runway, the operator simply pointed the scope at one side of the runway. The adjustment signal produced by this movement would then send the X-10 off the opposite side of the runway. The operator could then flee safely in the direction the Hero Scope was pointing.

Flight 1
The first attempt to fly X-10 number one [19307] was on 1 October 1953. During final countdown the ET-33 discovered a problem with the radio control system. The R/C stepping switch was not switching the aircraft to the turn mode. The flight was immediately canceled.

The clamshell nozzles of X-10 number one [GM19307] at Wright Patterson AFB Museum. The failure to open of the port engine nozzle forced the cancellation of the 13 October 1953 flight. These nozzles were to control engine exhaust flow. Today, modern fighters use 2D nozzles that widen and narrow in two directions Photo by: Author.

The second attempt to launch number one occurred on 2 October. High winds on the lake bed at the time of flight canceled this launch. This cancellation also exposed further problems with the radio control unit.

Problems with the radio control system prompted NAA engineers to perform a test of the F-45 voltage inverter unit. This test involved the connecting of one engine alternator directly to the radio control system. This test proved the problem was not in the F-45, but it also burned out the alternator.

As a result of this test both the alternators and the F-45 were replaced with improved units. The new F-45A inverter had a built in regulator to control output. This new equipment was subjected to a vibration test at Edwards AFB on 9 October 1953. The results were highly satisfactory.

With the new systems tested, on 13 October NAA again began its countdown for the first X-10 flight. This time however a new problem arose. During its final airborne check, the ET-33 commanded the left engine clamshell nozzle to close. The response was extremely slow and when the ET-33 commanded the nozzle to open it did not respond. Later it was discovered that the engine auxiliary electronic control had failed.

With the repairs completed, at midnight on 13 October NAA again began its countdown. No delays or unplanned holds occurred and at 09:20 AM PST on 14 October 1953 the chocks were released. Number one roared down Edwards EW runway, its nose pitched up 14 degrees.

Under the control of the ET-33A chase plane, the missile took off and climbed for altitude. Then came the first malfunction: the main gear doors failed to close. This malfunction was not enough to abort the flight however and the X-10 was allowed to accelerate to Mach 0.75 [440 knots]. Maximum altitude achieved was 20,900 feet.

During the flight difficulties arose with the ET-33's radio control unit's pitch command. Control of the missile was thus turned over to the ground station for a portion of the flight.

Control was then returned to the chase plane which then guided the X-10 back to Rogers Dry Lake for a successful landing. The total flight time was 31 minutes, 40 seconds and the total distance traveled was 195 miles.

The landing may have been successful but it left a few NAA engineers a little shaken. First the main gear failed to lock down until contact with the runway. As a result, it was not pressurized causing the main gear struts to bottom on contact. Then the pilot chute deployed late extending the ground run [eventual run 3.5 miles]. Finally, a clutch on the differential brakes failed. This last failure caused the brakes to be applied too long causing the near complete loss of tread on the left wheel and partial loss on the right.

The important fact of all this was that number one had flown and landed intact. The vehicle was stable in flight and almost everything was working properly.

Flight 2

The next attempt to get [19307] airborne occurred on 4 December 1953. This countdown lasted only five hours before winds and rain forced its cancellation.

The second attempt began the next day at two in the morning on Edwards AFB's EW runway. A number of minor item holds caused a delay, but at 15:04 the chocks were released. Thus, began the second flight of X-10 number one [19307].

In this flight X-10 number one took off under ground control to test the out-of-sight operating system. During climb out however the landing gear did not retract. The flight was not aborted however and X-10 number one climbed to an altitude of 24,400 feet and a speed of Mach 0.71. The ground control system then successfully headed the missile back to Rogers Dry Lake. Once there the ET-33 brought the vehicle in for landing. Total time for this flight, 35 minutes, 18 seconds.

A top view of number one in-flight. Again we see the vertical antenna and a complete lack of a stripe. Photo by: Rockwell International.

A color starboard quarter view of X-10 number one on the lake bed. The vehicle is in the later test colors of a long orange stripe and a small orange patch under the nose. This was not used in the early testing. Photo by: Rockwell International.

The failure to retract the landing gear was the only significant problem with this flight. North American engineers later determined that the problem was aerodynamic. As the vehicle climbed to cruise altitude, airflow past the landing gear doors began to produce lift. This lift was in opposition to the retraction force produced by the landing gear's hydraulics. Adding to the problem was the gyroscopic effect produced by the main gear wheels turning in the vehicle air flow. These two forces combined were too powerful for the hydraulic system, preventing retraction.

Initially NAA engineers solved the problem by keeping the vehicle speed down to between 185 and 200 MPH during gear retraction. Later a more specific solution to this problem was the addition of a special switch to the main landing gear strut. When the gear strut's shocks fully extended [immediately after liftoff], the switch would close automatically locking the wheel's brakes. With wheel rotation stopped, the gear was then quickly retracted before the vehicle reached 220 MPH.

Number one sits in its chocks on the lake bed. The engine nozzles are wide open and the canard is set in vertical pitch. The portable chocks were essential to the proper launching of the missile. The differential brakes were primarily for use in controlling the vehicle, not holding it on the ground. This chock unit had to release both main wheels instantly to prevent the missile veering right or left on takeoff. Note the tension wrinkles in the body skin. This picture was taken after the first flight. Photo By: Rockwell International.

Flight 3
On 15 December 1953 NAA again rolled number one out for a flight. Countdown began at 11:00 PM PST and proceeded normally until 5:45 AM 16 December [X-3:00]. At that point an oil line to the guidance compartment broke causing a hold. The line was quickly repaired and the countdown resumed at 6:45 AM. Then, just before flight, at 9:45 AM an electrical short occurred in the checkout electrical trailer. The short knocked out the trailer completely forcing the cancellation of the flight.

The trailer and the weather conspired to keep the next launch from occurring until 25 February 1954. This time X-10 Number One was to gather data on the vehicle's flight characteristics at transonic speeds [which required retracted landing gear]. This flight also was to test vehicle flutter in this speed range.

Countdown started at midnight and continued with minor delays until engine start. Then the telemetry system's

subcommutator and autocalibration unit failed. A hold was initiated until 12:00 Noon to repair the unit. Then, at 1:51 PM, X-10 Number One roared down Edwards AFB's "all weather runway" at south base.

Under the control of the ground system, Number One safely took off to the south east and properly retracted its main gear. It then headed towards its planned cruise altitude and its first try at the sound barrier. Four minutes into the flight however the telemetry systems five volt instrument supply failed. Now unable to gather data on the transonic region the flight was aborted.

Control was turned over to the ET-33 which flew the vehicle at subsonic speeds to burn up fuel. Maximum speed reached was only Mach 0.69 at an altitude of only 18,900 feet. The return flight was uneventful with the missile being landed by the ET-33 aircraft.[3]

The landing was a bit hard causing the pilot chute to deploy immediately and just as quickly fail. This produced a rather long ground run of 3.3 miles. The vehicle was not damaged and NAA personnel quickly transported it back to the hangar.

Flight 4
At midnight on 31 March 1954, the countdown began for GM19307's fourth flight. Like the previous flight, this was to study vehicle performance in the supersonic region. The vehicle was set up on the south lake bed's south shore runway [S-E]. A number of minor delays slowed the countdown, but at 1:51 PM PST number one again soared skyward.

Initially everything seemed to be going wrong. After take-off the right gear strut initially failed to retract. To accomplish retraction, the ground controller had to slow the vehicle down to 160 knots.

After this problem was corrected, the left engine appeared to be accelerating sluggishly. Then a pin on the radar's reference generator sheared making the radar and the plotting board intermittently useless. This last problem forced the ground controller to get his steering information from the F-100 chase plane.

Though still in flight testing, the F-100 Super Sabre was the fastest aircraft at Edwards in 1953. Regardless of this, the X-10 could easily outrun the Super Sabre.

All this activity was happening over a largely uninhabited area of California desert North-East of Edwards. This area was used for all secret testing in the 1950's.

Opposite: An F-100 Super Sabre in flight. This type of aircraft was the chase plane used in the number one's high speed run. According to an NAA engineer, the F-100 used in the flight was flown by North American's chief test pilot. When the X-10's afterburners were engaged and the vehicle accelerated to Mach 1.47, this pilot is stated to have yelled over the radio "Wait for Me." Though probably just engineering humor, the test pilot may actually have said this. With the radar system faulty and the ground controller using the test pilot's observations for control inputs, he may have been telling them to slow down before he lost track of the missile. Photo By: Rockwell International.

After all these problems were dealt with, ground control then ignited Number One's afterburners. Now under full power the vehicle quickly broke the sound barrier reaching a speed of Mach 1.47. The vehicle also reached 38,700 feet altitude, more than half way to the planned flight altitude of the WS-104A Navaho missile.

After its successful flight, Number One was returned to Edwards AFB. Because of the radar problems, landing was under the control of the ET-33 control aircraft. Landing was normal, though the pilot chute deployed late causing a landing run of 7,400 feet.

Even with all its problems, the flight was extremely productive. The telemetry system functioned properly sending quantitative data on vehicle performance and flutter. This data would be very useful in both the design of the Navaho G-38 missile and future aerospace vehicles.

Flight 5

On the evening of 4 May 1953, North American rolled out its second X-10 [GM19308] onto the south lake bed. Countdown began at midnight and at 11:07 AM on 5 May 1953 X-10 number two roared down the south shore runway.

The flight was to test the performance of the radio command system, radar tracker and the vehicle telemeter at extended ranges. This was in preparation for the later flights at the Air Force Missile Test Center at Cape Canaveral flights. The vehicle also was to gather data on landing gear operation.

After taking off towards the southeast X-10 Number Two was turned north. There it was flown as far as 100 nautical miles from its ground control station. Maximum speed achieved was Mach 0.77 with a flight altitude of 31,200 feet.

A rear side photo of number two [GM19308] in flight. Note the red engine exhaust area and red engine intakes. This color scheme was only used on this X-10, allowing it to be identified in any picture. Also note the vertical antenna like on number one. Photo By: National Archives.

The only significant problem with the flight was that the vehicle's tracking smoke generator failed. Otherwise the flight was perfect, with Number Two safely landing at Edwards AFB [slight delay in parabrake]. Total flight time was 72.5 minutes with a maximum distance of 427 nautical miles.

Flight 6

The countdown for GM19308's second flight began at 10:30 PM on 3 June 1954. Eighteen hours later, with a 25-30 knot quartering tail wind, at 4:28 PM on 4 June 1954 X-10 Number Two again took off from the south shore runway.

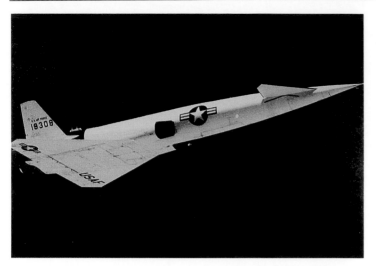

A lower front view of number two in-flight. Next to number one, X-10 number two is one of the most photographed X-10s. This is surprising considering it only flew three times. Photo By: National Archives.

This mission was to test missile performance in the supersonic region and the performance of the vehicle's parachute braking system. Unlike the previous flights however, this mission was doomed from the very start.

Shortly after chock release the missile veered to the left. Ground control brought the vehicle back on line almost immediately, but then halfway down the runway the left main gear tire failed. The remainder of the takeoff roll was completed on the wheel rim.

After takeoff the vehicle then failed to retract the damaged gear. Now incapable of its speed run the vehicle was accelerated to Mach 0.55 and flown to a parking altitude of 17,000 feet. Here it remained for a short time while NAA engineers examined the telemetry to see if the fault could be corrected from the ground. To hold the vehicle at this altitude and speed however required the intermittent use of the afterburners which greatly reduced the fuel reserve.

While the vehicle was in this holding pattern the five volt instrument bus failed. The emergency battery came on line but this would not last the whole flight. Thus, the decision was made to return the vehicle to Edwards AFB.

Landing approach was to the west towards Edwards AFB's E-W runway. Ground control then released number two to the ET-33 control aircraft. The ET-33 controller then gently landed the vehicle, sparing the main gear as much as possible. The vehicle's parabrake then failed and at approximately 0.7 miles down the runway the left strut failed.

The failure of the strut caused the vehicle to ground loop to the left. When it came to a stop the vehicle was resting on its left wing tip. Superficial damage was caused to the left wing tip, left elevon and the wing center section skin. The vehicle however was intact.

Flight 7

After repairs, at 10:30 PM PST on 30 June 1954 the countdown began for the third flight of X-10 Number Two. Several minor problems and adjustments slowed the count, but at

5:16 PM on 1 July 1954 GM19308 rolled down the runway. The goal of this flight: to test vehicle performance at supersonic speed and the parabraking system.

Takeoff, gear retraction and climb out were normal. Then, at about 17,500 feet, the airborne controller saw a long flame coming from the vehicle. Immediately the engines were returned to military power to see if the fire was from the afterburners. Quickly it became apparent that it was not the afterburners.

A lower rear shot of number two. The chase pilot reported a long flame coming from the engine exhaust area. It could have been only a minor problem with the afterburners [the J-40 engine was problem prone]. The tumbling of the gyros however made it impossible to save the vehicle. Later the F-86D flew the same profile and replicated the gyro tumble. The flight maneuver was noted to be avoided in future flights. Photo By: National Archives.

A destruct command was given, but the vehicle did not respond. The vehicle was then issued a left turn command to head the vehicle to the north. Because the vehicle was in a 20 degree up pitch, this command caused the autopilot's gyros to tumble. The vehicle pulled up in a steep climb, and then rolled left into a descending left turn.

Everything seemed to fail after that. No radio control due to the autopilot failure. The engines cutout, possibly due to the steep diving turn. Even the radio beacon failed.

Number Two leveled off at about 5,000 feet but continued descending. The missile then pancaked five miles south of Red Mountain east of Cuddeback lake. On landing Number Two hit the ground, bounced and then broke up and burned. It was the first X-10 lost in testing. The flight had only lasted 8 minutes 15 seconds.

The first impact produced a perfect impression of the vehicle's planform in the sand. As for the fire, it was so intense it actually ignited the missile's aluminum structure.

Flight 8

The loss of Number Two was disturbing, but it did not stop the testing program. At 11:15 PM, 11 August 1954 the countdown began for the first flight of vehicle Number Four

[GM19310]. This vehicle was the airborne structural test X-10, instrumented with strain gages to read structural loads while in-flight. Its mission was to prove the vehicle's structural integrity and obtain vibration data. The vehicle's glide brakes also were to be tested and data gathered on the automatic landing system.

Now officially the countdown started on 11 August, but in reality it did not start until much later. A leak in the main fuel tank's access door had forced the removal of the missile's engines. Installation then took until 1:30 AM on 12 August, at which time the countdown truly began.

X-10 GM-19307 [number one] takes off from the lake bed. Identification comes from the body strip running from engine exhaust to nose. This could have been any one of the second string of flights completed by number one. Photo By: Rockwell International.

Takeoff occurred at 1:48 PM on 12 August from Edwards E-W runway. Takeoff, gear retraction, and climb out were all normal. The vehicle reached its cruise altitude of 34,000 feet within seven minutes. During this climb the vehicle performed a structural demonstration maneuver.

Once at 34,000 feet number four was pitched downward and broke the sound barrier in a shallow dive. At reaching Mach 1.3 the missile was then pitched up and holding Mach climbed to 40,800 feet. Then power was reduced and the vehicle began a slow descent to Edwards.

At 20,000 feet the X-10's glide brakes were activated for the first time. The deceleration period proved longer then expected, forcing the test to be ended early for lack of time.

After the glide brake test the vehicle was brought in under the control of the ET-33. Landing was good and the parabrake functioned normally. The landing run was just 7,000 feet. Total flight time was 39 minutes 37 seconds.

The flight produced good results. Radio control and telemetry worked properly. The structural test also was successful and the glide brakes responded satisfactory. The only true problems were the failure of a fuel transfer test from tank three to tank two[5] and a Sundstrand alternator dropping in voltage for most of the flight.

Flight 9

On the evening of 1 September NAA again rolled Number One back out onto the south lake bed. Its initial test mission completed now it was replacing Number Two in the testing of the automatic approach and landing system. It also was to gather data on the landing gear. After a relatively good countdown, by morning bad weather had moved in forcing a major delay. The missile's radar altimeter also was experiencing interference [noise]. Thus, the countdown was ended and the launch rescheduled for the next day.

A front view of Number one on its belly after its successful wheels up landing. The working technicians give you a feel for the size of the vehicle. From their tans you also get an idea of how much time they have been spending on the lake bed. Note the holes in the side of the X-10, just in front of the Stars & Bars. Photo By: William F. Gibson Jr.

The new countdown started at 11:00 PM on 2 September. Several holds delayed the count by 7 hours 56 minutes. But at 3:40 PM on 3 September 1954 Number One [GM-19307] took off for the fifth time. Takeoff, gear retraction and climb out where normal. Most of the flight was over the isolated desert area Northeast of Edwards. Maximum speed was a slow Mach 0.44 and the maximum altitude was only 15,385 feet. To put it simply, number one took off eastward, circled Edwards counterclockwise and headed for a landing on the lake bed. It was here that something went wrong.

The first failure was the ground radar tracking system. This failure ended any chance of landing the missile using the automatic system. Then came the more ominous failure: the landing gear would not extend. Later investigation showed that the nose wheel hydraulic system had been connected backwards.

Unwilling to give up on Number One, the engineers decided to try a wheels up landing on the lake bed. Under the control of the ET-33 chase aircraft, Number One made a perfect wheels up landing. A major factor in this successful landing was the missile's delta wing which produced a strong landing ground effect, cushioning the impact. Damage was limited to the under side and forward bulkhead of the vehicle's number two fuel tank.

A rear view of number one on its belly. Note the multiple holes in the side of the X-10. From this photo you see that the cutting operation was more scattered then the narration indicates. There is even an ax cut in the middle of the Stars & Bars. Also note the parabrake unit sitting on top of the engine compartment. Photo By: William F. Gibson Jr.

The story of Number One's belly landing does not end here. By design, if an X-10's engines stopped running the destruct package would fire in thirty seconds. During normal landings, the engines ran at idle until an Air Force sergeant disarmed the destruct unit. Access to the unit was through the nose gear wheel well.[6]

For this landing however the sergeant had to drive all the way out to the south lake bed. He then had to stand in front of the air ducts of the running engines and cut an access hole into the X-10's port side with an ax. And as he did this, fuel from the damaged fuel tank was flowing out around his feet.

The situation did not end when the sergeant reached into

Number one back on its wheels and in its hangar at south base. The hanger was shared by the Bell X-1A rocket plane used by Chuck Yeager to exceed Mach 2.0. Again, note the holes cut into the vehicle's side by the Air Force Sergeant. The fact to remember is that the body skin of the X-10 was stainless steel. This gives the ax cutting operation over a pool of spilled jet fuel new meaning. Photo By: William F. Gibson Jr.

the hole. Whether he realized he had cut into the wrong side, or he could not get a good grip on the unit is not known. What is known however is that he suddenly moved to the starboard side of Number One and cut a second hole into the missile. It was through this hole that he disarmed the destruct package. Only then was X-10 Number One secure.

Flight 10

On 28 September 1954 Number Four (GM-19310) took off for the second time. Its test mission was the same as its previous flight: to show the structural integrity and supersonic performance of the X-10 design. It also was to test the automatic approach and landing system.

The vehicle performed its structural and supersonic flight test superbly with a new maximum speed of Mach 1.84 and a new altitude of 40,900 feet. It also functioned properly in its automatic approach sequence [a closed loop]. On landing however the automatic landing system made a catastrophic error and determined that landing flare should occur 20 feet below the runway. The vehicle hit like a brick and was completely destroyed.

Flight 11

On 1 December 1954 Number One was again back in the air. Again, its mission was to test the automatic approach and landing system. It also was to test lateral control on landing.

Because, the flight was to test the landing system maximum speed was only Mach 0.54 and the flight took less than 16 minutes. Yet the flight was extremely significant, for Number One both approached and landed successfully under automatic control. The only failure was that the vehicle rolled off the simulated Air Force Missile Test Center runway it landed on.

Flight 12

On 16 December, less than 15 days after its last flight, Number One was again airborne. This flight could be titled rerun since it reads almost exactly like the previous flight.

Its mission was the same as before, with the minor addition of testing lateral control during takeoff. Maximum speed was Mach 0.55 and the maximum altitude was only 21,500 feet. The vehicle successfully approached and landed on the simulated AFMTC runway and then rolled off as before.

Flight 13

On 22 February 1955 X-10 Number Five [GM-19311] took to the air for the first time. Its mission was to test the vehicle's performance at intermediate supersonic speeds and the closed loop approach and automatic landing system. This X-10 flight was also to test the missile's fuel transfer system: all previous flights flown used the number two [main] fuel tank only.

Takeoff and climb out was nominal but at the start of the speed run both afterburners failed. Maximum speed was Mach 0.94 with a maximum altitude of 41,800 feet [a record]. The only test that the vehicle could now do was the closed loop approach and automatic landing system.

Number one takes off during a later mission. Here we see the full undercarrlage of the missile. Photo By: Rockwell International.

During approach the vehicle suddenly stopped descending at about 100 feet over the lake bed. Radio control was implemented but the vehicle continued to hold altitude. Lake bed winds then caused the vehicle to drift off the simulated runway and over the North American support vehicles. At this point it was determined that the vehicle was stuck in a specific flight mode.

Control was turned over to the ET-33A aircraft. The airborne controller then placed the vehicle on to the proper approach course for the simulated runway. Then, just before landing, the parabrake deployed. Almost instantly the vehicle went nose first into the lake bed.

Flight 14

On 11 March 1955 North American rolled X-10 Number Three [GM-19309] out for flight testing. Originally the static test article for the X-10 program, the vehicle now had engines, hydraulics, and full subsystems.

Number three exploding during takeoff. This is an enlargement of a section of a picture taken. from the far end of the runway. In the original picture the ET-33 chase plane can also be seen. Photo By: William F. Gibson Jr.

Like other flights, Number Three was to test the closed loop and automatic landing system. It also was to test a new radio command system and the transient programmer. Engine ignition was normal and the vehicle roared down the runway. At 164 knots the wheels left the runway and missile began its climb out. The control system then commanded the landing gear to retract.

The instant the gear began retraction, X-10 Number Three exploded. What had happened was that during the installation of the new radio control system the destruct package had been wired to the gear system instead of the vehicle engines. When the wheel shocks fully extended, instead of locking the brakes it triggered the explosives.

Flight 15

On 24 March 1955 North American rolled out X-10 Number One once more on to Rogers Dry Lake. Again the mission was to test the automatic approach and landing system and lateral control during both takeoffs and landings.

Ground control handled both takeoff, climb out, and cruise phases of the flight. Control was then turned over to the automatic approach and landing systems that brought Number

Number one on landing. A fitting end for the X-10 test flights at Edwards. Photo By: Rockwell International.

One down perfectly for the third time. This time however the X-10 did not leave the simulated Air Force Missile Test Center runway. Thus, Number One finally proved that the X-10s could operate from Cape Canaveral.

Flight 15 was the last of the Edwards test flights. As originally planned, the flight test program now moved to the AFMTC at Cape Canaveral. There the X-10s could reach Mach 2 and maximum range and not have them fly over civilian areas. The planned dive in attack method also could be tested against certain islands located within the test range.

The Edwards Flights, Summary

The X-10 flights at Edwards were very important, both to the Navaho program and to aerospace history.

The fifteen flights produced the following results for the Navaho program.

(1) That the vehicle's structure could stand speeds up to Mach 1.84.

(2) That the vehicle's PIX10 autopilot could keep the vehicle in stable, level, flight at supersonic speeds. The autopilot also could carry out course and speed changes as set by ground control.

(3) The successful development of the auto approach and landing system. Though it was not always successful, the X-10 had landed on a runway the size of the one at the Air Force Missile test Center, Florida.

(4) Successful testing of the telemetry system.

(5) Initial testing of the missile fuel transfer system. This was needed for the longer range Cape flights.

(6) Testing of the vehicle's glide brakes.

In addition to these technological developments the X-10 flights also set some records, though not official since no man piloted the vehicles.

On 28 September 1954, X-10 Number Four [GM19310] achieved a speed of Mach 1.84. Even at Edwards AFB, the home of the rocket planes, this was a major aerospace achievement. On that day the X-10 became the fastest turbojet powered vehicle in the world.

The flight to Mach 1.47 in April had maxed out the F-100, the fastest United States fighter in service in 1954. The flight to Mach 1.84 beat out everything else that used a turbine for propulsion. Neither the XF-102 or the XF-104 aircraft could not match the X-10's speed [the XF-102 could not even exceed Mach 1].

The only vehicles faster then the X-10 were the rocket planes and a drone called the X-7. Manned rocket planes had reached Mach 2.44 and the X-7 had reached Mach 3. The difference however was that only the X-10 could takeoff and land conventionally [under its own power]. These vehicles had to be air launched from a mother ship/bomber at about 20,000 feet.

One test pilot reportedly stated " if North American would put a saddle on it [a cockpit] he would fly it (the X-10)." Unfortunately, in 1954 flight control systems were not up to man rating this vehicle.

NOTES

(1) RTV-A-5 was a government identification code. In the RASCAL program, the Shrike sub-scale test vehicle was designated RTV-A-4. The NATIV also has been reported to have been designated RTV-A-3.

(2) This is man rating. All man rated military aircraft are structurally designed to survive 1.5 times the maximum aerodynamic load expected during flight.

(3) The ET-33 also suffered a failure during this flight. After emptying its auxiliary fuel tanks, it could not jettison one before landing. The result was that it was more difficult to land the ET-33 then the X-10.

(4) It is worth noting that X-10 Number One [GM-19307] shared its hanger with Bell's X-1A rocket aircraft. This was the fastest aircraft in the world at the time.

(5) For all the X-10 flights, the vehicles flew on the fuel carried in tank two.

(6) In reverse, the arming of the X-10's destruct package was done with the engines running. During the takeoff count down the Air Force sergeant would drive up to the vehicle on the runway and arm the system. Then he would quickly leave before the count down reached zero and the engines were brought to full power.

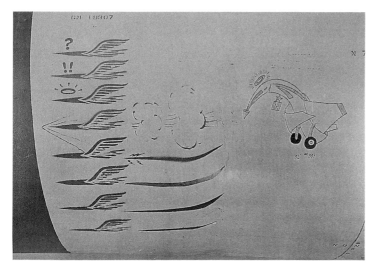

A special cartoon that was painted on the side of number one by a North American artist. It shows all the flights made by number one. Behind the flight silhouettes is a cartoon of number one taking a bow. Around its neck is a medal saying hero. Unfortunately, after being delivered to the Air Force Museum the cartoon was painted over and lost. Photo By: William F. Gibson Jr.

Chapter 3

WS-104A, Phase Two & Three

The G-26

A year after the Air Force inspected the X-10 mockup, in June 1952 North American Aviation unveiled the G-26. The role of this vehicle in the Navaho program was to prove the vertical launch system and the piggyback booster arrangement. It also was to gather data on supersonic flight beyond Mach 2.5. North American would then use this information to refine the final vehicle, the G-38.

Approving of the mockup, on 23 December 1952 the Air Force issued North American the G-26 Design, Fabrication, and Test contract. This contract called for the construction of ten missiles, 13 boosters, and five N-6 autonavigators. Construction of the first unit was to begin in 1953 with the first launch in February of 1956.

SPECIFICATIONS [G-26]

Missile

Length:	67' 9"	Wing Span:	28' 7"
Height:	9' 6"	Weight:	65,000 lbs.

Booster

Length:	76' 3"	Weight:	25,000 lbs.

Diameter:	5' 10"

Performance

Missile

Speed:	Mach 2.75	Altitude:	55,000' to 80,000'
Range:	3,500 miles		

Booster

Altitude of engine burnout:	43,000'
Altitude of vehicle separation:	48,000'

Propulsion

Missile: Two XRJ47-W-5 Wright Aeronautical Ramjets
Maximum Thrust - 15,000 lbs.

Booster: Two XLR83-NA-1 liquid fuel rocket engines
Maximum Thrust - 240,000 lbs.

Guidance

Missile: N6A inertia guidance unit with PIX10 autopilot

Booster: Controlled by missile guidance unit

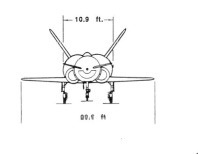

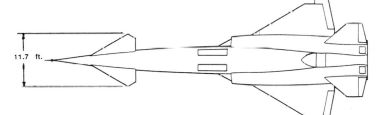

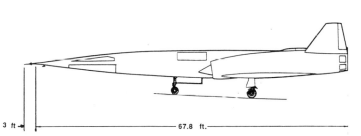

A three view drawing of the G-26 flight missile with dimensions. Photo by: William F. Gibson Jr.

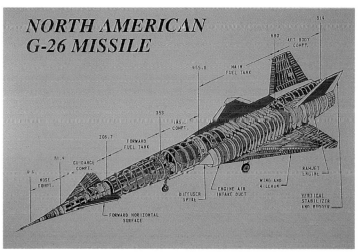

A colorized cutaway of the G-26 missile. Here we see the internal layout of the flight missile. Starting at the nose are the antenna and guidance compartments. Then the forward fuel tank followed by the instrument compartment. Then comes the engine intakes and main fuel tank followed by the ramjets in the aft fuselage. Photo by: Author.

The Missile

The G-26 missile looked extremely similar to the X-10. It was of the same delta/canard configuration, and almost exactly the same physical dimensions. It did have notched wing tips, and its twin tails were placed further back on the body. If you were not looking closely however, you could not tell the two vehicles apart.

The real difference between the two vehicles was internal. A good starting point is the engine nacelles within which were 48 inch diameter supersonic ramjets. These were the largest ramjets produced during the 1950s, possibly the largest ramjets ever flown. Development was by the Wright Aeronautical Corporation, a company that can trace it's roots to the Wright brothers.

The use of ramjets resulted in some design differences between the X-10 and G-26. Because of its ramjet engines, to slow the G-26 in-flight the vehicle had air brakes positioned around the engine exhaust nozzle. These brakes were used in flight and during landing.

Another difference was the G-26's F-104 style spiked diffuser. Though less efficient than the converging/diverging system used on the X-10, this type of diffuser is more reliable. It also simulated the planned multi-shock spiked inlet the G-38 vehicle was to use.

The last major change caused by the ramjets was the mounting of an Auxiliary Power Unit [APU] in the bulge between the twin tails. Unlike a turbojet which can drive a generator, ramjets have no moving parts or a drive shaft. Thus, the APU was needed to generated all the electrical power used by the G-26 during the flight.

Other changes included the moving of the instrument/warhead compartment aft to the engine ducts. This allowed engineers to enlarge the forward fuel tank. NAA engineers also enlarged the main tank by incorporating both the third and fourth fuel tanks. This reduced the complexity of the missile's fuel transfer system.

Along with these compartment changes, the G-26 also used titanium in its structure. One of the first aircraft to use this metal, NAA engineers used Titanium in high temperature areas like the nose and the ramjet exhaust. At an altitude of 70,000 feet a missile traveling at a sustained speed of Mach 2.75 will have a skin temperature of 520 degrees Fahrenheit.

The final change was subtle. On the X-10, North American made the nose wheel gear strut extremely long. This was so the vehicle had a five degree up angle-of-attack during takeoff roll. On the vertically launched G-26 there was no need for this. Thus, the G-26's nose wheel strut was so short its nose pointed down [negative pitch] when it was on the ground.

The Booster

Of course, a major difference between the X-10 and the G-26 was the booster. This was a large aluminum [20-24ST] liquid fuel rocket unit. Longer than the flight missile, its purpose was to get the missile up to 43,000 feet and a speed of Mach 3.

From the nose to the center of the separation fin is the LOX tank [Liquid Oxygen]. This section was primarily monocoque1 structure with structural longerons beginning at the forward missile attachment fitting. Tank pressurization was by gaseous oxygen [GOX] which boiled off from the Liquid Oxygen. To reduce heat transfer to the cryogenic liquid dur-

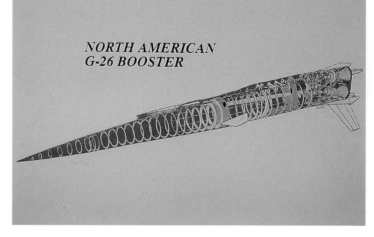

NORTH AMERICAN G-26 BOOSTER

A colorized cutaway drawing of the G-26 booster. Taken from an engineering drawing of the booster we can see the forward LOX tank, then the Kerosene tank [with helium spheres] and then the engine section. Photo by: Author.

ing flight, this section also was coated with fiberglass honeycomb insulation.

Directly behind the LOX tank was the alcohol tank [see Development – Booster]. A semi-monocoque structure, it carried most of the weight of the flight missile. Pressurization was by helium gas carried in small spherical bottles carried inside the fuel tank.

The final section was the engine housing. Here were two 120,000 pound thrust Liquid oxygen and Alcohol rocket engines: total thrust 240,000 pounds. Also here were the two vertical tails that helped to stabilize the vehicle in flight. Like the separation fins, these were non-movable aerodynamic surfaces.

The booster was responsible for both takeoff thrust and flight control below supersonic speed. Mounted in the engine bells were graphite thrust vectoring vanes. These vanes produce changes in the vehicles flight path by changing the angle of thrust of the engines. This was the only means of flight control until the vehicle reached a high enough speed to make the missile's aerodynamic surfaces functional.

Constructing the booster resulted in several new technologies. To reduce weight while retaining the required structural strength, engineers developed a chemical milling process for the booster's skin. Called Chem-Milling, an acid bath gradually removes metal from a metal object. In the case of the G-26 booster, North American used the process to reduce the interior of 0.125 inch thick 20-24ST skin panels while maintaining the thickness of the weld lands. This milling is incredibly accurate, allowing precise dimensions.

A more advanced version of Chem-Mill allows for the etching of the material to produce complex surface patterns. By masking portions of the metal panel with an acid resistant coating, engineers can produce integrally-stiffened structure. This gives the panel the required structural strength at minimal weight.

Another advance came from the need to weld 20-24ST aluminum. This strong [structural] aluminum alloy could not be welded using methods then in service. North American developed an automated inert gas tungsten arc fusion welding process. Now called "Heliarc" welding, this system allowed for the welding of the skin panels. It was first used to weld G-26 panels in May of 1952.

Development, G-26 Missile

The G-26 was in truth a variant of the X-10. Though designed for higher speeds, its aerodynamic shape mirrored the X-10. As a result, its development rested primarily on the success of the X-10 flight test program. North American in fact did not release the design for production until the X-10 had successfully flown supersonic.

An Air Force Development and Engineering Inspection team reviewed the G-26 missile in March of 1954. The next month the X-10 flew to Mach 1.47, proving the aerodynamic design. Regardless of this however, North American Aviation would not release the detailed design for the G-26 until August.

Construction of the first G-26 missile began soon after the design release. The first airframe completed [the G-26 static test article] was vehicle number three. In January, NAA engineers placed this airframe in the Horizontal Test Fixture previously used to test the X-10 [see WS-104A, Phase One, The X-10]. The Testing procedure was the same however, the loading problem was more difficult due to the higher temperatures. One result of this greater difficulty was the accidental breaking of the vehicle's keel beam during a test run.

While development of the G-26 airframe was underway, three other programs were in progress that were essential for this vehicle. First, was the development of powerful ramjet engines, the largest yet conceived. Second, was the development of an Auxiliary Power Unit capable of powering the missiles electronics and hydraulics. Third and last was the development of an effective autonavigator unit.

The Ramjets

Ramjets were by far the newest form of jet engine, the first being tested in Germany during the war. These early ramjets were rigid in thrust and could only operate in a very narrow air speed range. Try to ignite one at too slow a speed and it would not ignite. Try flying one at too high a speed and the air flow through the engine would blow it out like a candle.

To put it mildly, the ramjet was the most under developed of all three jet engine types available in 1950. The largest American ramjet at the time was just 4 inches in diameter [and subsonic]. To go from this to a huge 40 inch plus design that worked at Mach three was not going to be easy.

These issues were well understood by Wright Aeronautical. Since the end of the war they had been studying ramjets, as part of the earlier MX-770/XSSM-A-2 program. In October of 1950 NAA gave the G-26 ramjet development contract to Wright Aeronautical. Seven months later, in May of 1951 North

G-26 flight missile number 14 awaits completion at North American Aviation's Downey facility. Note the jack placed under the guidance section [Canard]. This jack allowed the vehicle to remain level during assembly. Without it, the short nose wheel would produce a noticeable nose droop. Also, note the Navaho logo on the side of the missile. Photo by: NAA Chronology.

G-26 number 11 is rolled out of the Downey assembly area. The tails of the missile were so tall that the landing gear had to be retracted and the missile pulled out on a low dolly to clear the doorway. The large, four foot diameter, ramjets have not yet been installed. Even today, these are the largest ramjets to have ever flown. Photo by: William F. Gibson Jr.

American established the performance requirements for the engines.

With the requirements established detailed design began in July of 1951. Wright Aeronautical then delivered its first engine mockup in March of 1952. The next month, the X-7 drone began testing a 20 inch prototype engine. Designated the XRJ47-W-1, this small engine would fly seven times on this drone aircraft. Only one of these flights was successful; three were partially successful.

In February of 1953 the prototype fuel control system for the ramjets was flight tested. Several months later, in August NACA technicians performed the first pipe test on a full size XRJ47-W-5 engine. NACA then began the testing program for the engine burners in January of 1954.

In May of 1954 tunnel tests began on a heavy duty version of the G-26 ramjet engine. Two months later, in July of 1954 Wright released the engine's detailed design for production. The first pair of engines was then accepted by the Air Force in June of 1955.

The APU

Because the G-26 was propelled by ramjets, it needed an auxiliary power unit to produce electricity and hydraulic power for the missile's flight systems. To accomplish this Marquardt proposed a ram air turbine unit. As the G-26 flew through the atmosphere, air would flow around it at high speed. Like a small windmill, the air turbine would use some of this air flow to produce electricity and hydraulic power. Many years later the United States Army used such a device to power its Corporal II missile.

The problem with the air turbine however was that the vehicle had to be moving for it to work. This meant that it produced no power at launch or the first few minutes of flight.

A photo of the rear of an unidentified G-26 still being assembled at Downey. The airbrakes are open as is the parachute door. Just to the side of the parachute door is the exhaust port for the APU which was in front of the chute. Its proximity to the right vertical tail was the source of concern for NAA engineers. The danger was that the APU exhaust would overheat the rudder surface. Photo by: NAA Chronology.

For it to work the engineers would have to install a battery system to provide power to the vehicle's avionics at takeoff. This added weight was unacceptable and in July 1953 NAA canceled the turbine.

Now without an APU North American began asking for new proposals. Three months later, in October NAA signed a contract with the Walter Kidde Company. Their APU used the decomposition of ethylene Oxide to produce a high temperature gas. This gas was then sent to a turbine which in turn ran an alternator and a hydraulic pump. Once the process started, it would continue until the APU exhausted its fuel.

The Walter Kidde APU was not trouble free. The glow plug that maintained the reaction tended to electrically ground out. The turbine, which ran at 78,000 RPMs, had bearing problems. There also was regular concern over the APU exhaust plume over-heating the G-26's vertical stabilizer. Throughout the G-26 program the APU would prove a liability.

Auto Navigation

N-2

Nothing has been said about the autonavigation unit since Chapter One. The development of a functional autonavigator was essential to the success of the G-26 program. Without such a unit the final missile, the G-38, would not be possible.

Before the WS-104A program began, in May of 1950 North American began flight testing the XN-1 autonavigator. By March of 1951 28 flights had been completed using a C-47 [DC-3] aircraft. These tests proved the N-1 unit which was the baseline for the stellar inertial XN-2.

Laboratory testing of the XN-2's star tracker began in June of 1951. Daylight testing then began in July with North American mounting the unit in a large Van. These tests were completed in February of 1952.

With the van tests completed on 1 March 1952, the first daylight flight was completed using a YC-97 aircraft. In all 22

G-26 number 14 again, this time at a different angle. Note the port just in front of the Navaho logo used in the fueling of the forward fuel tank. Seen in the background are several unfinished G-26 booster units Photo by: NAA Chronology

flights were completed, the last on 31 May 1953. These tests proved the viability of the stellar inertial design.

Prior to the completion of the XN-2 flight tests, in March of 1953 the first XN-2B unit was completed. Laboratory tests of this unit began in July with van testing beginning soon after. These van tests were completed in April of 1954 at which time all work on the XN-2 was abandoned.

N-6

The reason for the abandonment of the XN-2 was not that it was flawed. What had happened was that guidance technology had out paced it. And that technology was in the form of the N-6 fully inertial navigation unit.

While development of the XN-2 was underway, in May of 1951 North American engineers formulated a new guidance system design. This new guidance system design used six gyros instead of the normal three. The gyros were paired, two to an axis, and then connected to a digital computer.

The paired gyros rotated in opposition to each other. This way as one gyro's rotation induced precession caused it to deviate in one direction, the other gyro's precession was in the opposite direction. The computer would note the discrepancy and produce an adjustment. The result was a tremendous increase in accuracy.

This design was called NAVAN which officially stood for North American Vehicle Auto-Navigation. Unofficially the name was chosen because it was spelled the same way forward and backwards. A verbal representation of the forward and backward rotating gyro's.

The basic design of the N-6's computer was completed in March of 1952. Later that year the XN-2's air bearing gyros and KDIAs were replaced with new hydrodynamic bearing gyros. Advanced development of the N-6 then began in May of 1953.

Flight testing of the XN-6 began in May of 1954. The vehicle used in this test was a Convair T-20, an aircraft used to train Navy navigators. Testing of this unit would continue until the first X-10 N-6 test in 1956. The most notable test of the XN-6 occurred in April of 1955. For five consecutive days in that month the XN-6 was operated without a single malfunction.

While testing was underway, in June of 1954 NAA and the Air Force agreed that the Navaho would use the N-6. Development then began on a transistorized digital computer to reduce weight, size and improve reliability. Functional tests of this new computer began in May of 1955 with completion in July.

Development, G-26 Booster

Where development of the G-26 missile was coupled to the X-10 program, development of the booster was coupled to the design of powerful rocket engines. When the WS-104A program began North American had already developed a new 75,000 pound thrust engine. To meet the requirements of the G-26 however, NAA had to take the design further: to 120,000 pounds.

A G-26 booster is raised into the static test tower [Vertical Test Facility]. The tarp hanging down from the nose insured that anyone passing the facility along an adjacent road would only see a long rectangular sheet. The airport tower like building next door used to be a control tower when the facility had an on site airstrip. Photo by: William F. Gibson Jr.

To make this new engine required major advances in all aspects of rocket engine design. The turbopumps had to be more powerful while also being lightweight. The cooling system for the engines combustion chamber also had to be improved.

As part of this research, in June of 1951 the 75,000 pound thrust engine was run at 96,000 pounds for 6 seconds.

Development of the new engine began in mid-1951. In March NAA began a design study for a turbopump to power the 120,000 pound thrust engine. By August the design of the turbopump's gas generator was completed.

A gas generator rocket design is quite common. In this system a small amount of the rocket's fuel is siphoned off to the gas generator. Here the fuel is ignited, the resulting high temperature gas being then sent to a turbine. This turbine drives a pump – hence, turbopump – which pumps the propellant to the engine's combustion chamber. Keep all this in mind during the G-26 testing section.

The booster static test article in the test tower. Note the whiffle trees all over the booster. During tests the unit was filled with water to simulate fuel. Photo by: William F. Gibson Jr.

A G-26 booster in the tower. The lack of whiffle trees and other testing equipment might indicate that this picture is of the other side of the vertical testing facility. One side was used for the static testing of the booster. The other side was used for final checkout of boosters prior to their shipment to the Cape. Photo by: William F. Gibson Jr.

While work on the turbopump was underway, in June of 1951 preliminary design began on a new style lightweight tubular combustion chamber. In the old V-2s the thrust chamber was made of two sheets of metal forming a double walled combustion chamber. During engine burn the void between the chamber walls was filled with liquid oxygen. This cryogenic liquid kept the engine combustion chamber from melting under the intense heat.

In NAA's new design a series of tubes, bent to the configuration of the chamber and then brazed together, formed the chamber wall. This design enhanced the cooling effect, allowing a higher temperature combustion. This higher temperature combustion in turn improved engine efficiency and increased thrust and impulse. All later high thrust U.S. engines use this tubular design.

With these sub-programs well underway, in December of 1951 preliminary design of the G-26 booster was completed. Detailed design began the next month and in May of 1952 the first static firing of a 120,000 pound thrust engine was completed. In June the booster mockup was inspected by the Air Force and in October the first true G-26 engine [tubular bell] was assembled. Two months later, in December of 1952, the detailed structural design for the missile was released. The next month everything changed.

REAP [Rocket Engine Enhancement Program]

With testing of 120,000 pound thrust engines in progress, and design of a 405,000 pound thrust engine underway, in January of 1953 NAA's rocket propulsion group began an advanced propulsion research project. Called REAP [Rocket Engine Advancement Program] its purpose was to investigate ways of advancing rocket engine technology. The goal was to improve upon the first Navaho engine which was viewed as the state of the art in liquid fuel propulsion.

REAP revolutionized the G-26 and G-38 booster's by changing the fuel from Liquid Oxygen and Alcohol to Liquid Oxygen/Kerosene. This new fuel combination produced more thrust per gallon used than the previous fuel. It assured the booster would have enough power to carry its missile to 60,000 feet altitude. It also set the primary rocket fuel for the later Thor, Jupiter and Atlas missile's.

As a result of REAP the structural design of the G-26 had to be revised. The new design was not released until June of

Another picture of a G-26 in what appears to be the final checkout facility. According to NAA engineers during this final inspection a man was lower on a cable through the LOX vent into the LOX tank. There he used a flashlight to check for any loose bolts, rivets, or other foreign material left in the tank during assembly. Any such object could create LOX sensitivity, in which when the tank is filled the slightest shock could cause an explosion. Photo by: William F. Gibson Jr.

(A)

A series of views of the damage caused by the booster failure. (A) The rupture in the LOX tank. (B) Signs of the tank implosion in the nose of the booster. Next Page: (C) A good view of the Whiffle trees used to simulate launch loads. (D) A huge crease in the side of the booster caused by the weight of air.

(B)

1954. Static testing of the first booster then began in December following completion of the test tower.

During static testing at Downey, in March of 1955 the static test article was destroyed in a test run. The booster was undergoing a simulated launch loading when it failed at the mounting point for the missile. This failure cracked the liquid oxygen tank causing the fluid inside [water for the test] to drain out like a torrent.

As the water drained out, a low pressure area [a vacuum] was created in the upper portion of the booster. As the inside pressure dropped the booster's skin, designed to hold pressure in, began undergoing reverse loading. Within a moment the weight of a half an atmosphere of air crushed the upper portion of the booster [imploded].

Many years later, a nuclear armed Titan 1 would suffer a similar implosion style failure. This problem of fluid leakage

(C)

On 11 January of 1955, the Air Force issued a second G-26 production contract. This contract called for the construction of 12 more G-26 missiles, 21 boosters and six N6 autonavigators. This brought the total to 22 missiles, 34 boosters and 11 inertial guidance units.

The G-26 contracts showed that the Air Force only intended that half the missiles carry a N6A autonavigator. The remaining vehicles would be radio controlled from the ground. The radio control system had not been specified, but it is reasonable to believe that it used the X-10's radio control system.

The Intervening Years

While development and testing of the X-10 and G-26 missiles was underway, several important events occurred. These events would greatly affect the Navaho program, particularly the development of the G-38 missile.

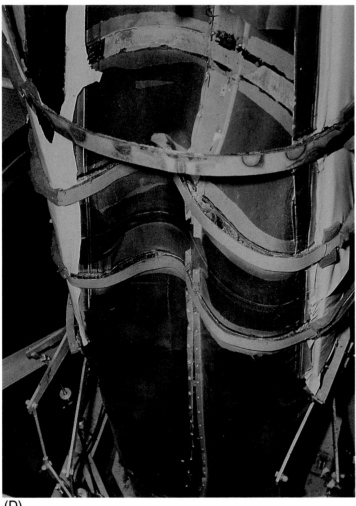

(D)

The detonation of a Mk-6 size warhead. Though extremely colorful, it also is deadly. The rusty brown color means it has large amounts of soil in the mushroom cloud. This soil will later rain down as radioactive fallout. The Navaho originally was to carry a warhead of this yield. Photo by: National Atomic Museum.

causing an implosion is inherent in all liquid fuel booster systems. It is just one reason why modern military missiles are solid fueled.

Four months after the destruction of the static test article a fully engined G-26 booster was static fired at Santa Susanna for 15 seconds. This test verified the booster's structure strength. This test also was the longest test of the developed engine.

Warhead Issues

Soon after the Navaho program became WS-104A the Air Force selected the W-4 warhead as its warhead. By the end of 1951, the Air Force had replaced the W-4[2] with the W-13. This new warhead stretched the limits of the X-10 and G-26 warhead section, but it would fit. It also increased the yield to 100 kilotons, increasing the Navaho's effectiveness.

The changes in the Navaho's warhead however, were just beginning. To regain its nuclear superiority over the Soviet Union, on 1 November 1952 the United States detonated its first hydrogen bomb. Code named Shot Mike of Operation Ivy, this device produced an explosion equal to 10.5 million tons of TNT.

The development of thermonuclear weapons had a major effect on the Navaho program. When the Mike shot occurred, one out of every two G-38s was to carry its bomb to within 1,500 feet of its target. This rather short miss distance was necessary to insure the destruction of the target area. If the warhead was the yield of the Mike device however, the acceptable miss distance increased to 10,000 feet. With this leeway, the earlier N2 guidance unit was an effective guidance unit. With the N6 autonavigator, a megaton class Navaho missile could destroy the hardest of targets.

Though the development of thermonuclear warheads had reduced the Navaho's guidance problem, it created a major payload problem. The Mike device was a test device, not a weapon prototype. The warhead unit alone was twenty feet long, six feet in diameter, and weighed 65 tons [130,000 pounds]. In addition, the unit had a cyrogenic support system that was larger than the whole G-26 missile/booster assembly.

Though the Mike device was not deployable, soon after its detonation, the United States tested the Super ORalloy [Mk-18] bomb. Though not as powerful as the Mike device [500 Kt], the Navaho only had to get it within 3,500 feet of its target. The problem was that the Mk-18 weighed over 10,000 pounds, greater than the G-26 could carry.[3] Until someone resolved this weight problem however, the Navaho warhead continued to be the W-13 fission device.

The Russian H Bomb

Before the Mike test was a year old, on 12 August 1953 the Soviet Union detonated its first thermonuclear device. This event stunned the United States government and military more than the Soviet's first nuclear bomb. Not only had they tested an H bomb, their bomb was deliverable.

The Soviets were developing an H bomb before they detonated their first atomic bomb. The development of the Soviet atomic bomb was in fact only a technological step necessary for the later H bomb. Thus, the speed of their development of a deliverable H bomb is not surprising.

Regardless of this, the fact they had a deliverable device caused a near panic in Washington. Before the year ended, the United States government allocated additional funds for the development of both a deliverable Hydrogen bomb and the missiles to carry it.

Another small or kiloton yield detonation. These early low yield warheads pushed the development of highly accurate guidance systems. Photo by: National Atomic Museum.

The Final Changes

Overnight the Navaho had to carry a thermonuclear device. This was a difficult task to accomplish. The weaponized version of the Mike device [the EC-16] weighted 30 tons [60,000 pounds]. The EC-14, a solid fueled H bomb, weighted as much as 29,000 pounds. Neither the G-26 or the then planned G-38 could carry any of these warheads.

Regardless of the Navaho's payload limitations, the Air Force was not willing to give up on this missile. The reason was simple: the Navaho did not have to escape the blast of an H bomb, a manned bomber did. Thus, the Air Force issued a request for a lightweight thermonuclear device.

On 22 January 1954 North American Aviation completed a Weapon System Optimization study. In this study, NAA engineers considered several fission and fusion warheads for the X-10/G-26 size missiles. The results were that these missiles could only carry the XW-12, XW-5, and XW-13 fission devices. On the fusion side, only the in development XW-15 was small enough to fit.

It was in this report that North American then proposed an enlarged missile called the B-64A. This vehicle could carry

The Romeo bomb blast is a brilliant red on a blue black background. This hydrogen device was detonated on 26 March 1954, soon after the Bravo shot. Called the Runt, it produced a larger than expected 11 megaton blast. Within one minute its mushroom cloud was six miles across and had reached an altitude of 44,000 feet. It was this kind of power that made it possible to destroy hardened military targets with miss distances of one mile. Photo by: Los Alamos National Laboratories.

The Mike blast of Operation Ivy produces a huge white mushroom. Though a successful tests of a fusion device, the unit was impossible to carry even by the massive B-36 bomber. Only with the development of solid, high yield, small hydrogen warheads was the ICBM possible. Photo by: Los Alamos National Laboratories.

a 10,000 pound payload [15,000 pounds for reduced ranges] in its 148 inch long, 70 inch diameter payload bay. At this payload a high yield H bomb was achievable. The Air Force accepted this design change and on 24 September 1954 canceled the XW-13 warhead. This enlarged vehicle became the G-38.

BRAVO

Soon after North American submitted its report, on 1 March 1954 the United States detonated its second thermonuclear bomb. Code named Shot Bravo of Operation Castle, it was the first test of a solid fuel H bomb design. The explosion would become famous for its power.

Though the scientists called the device the Shrimp, its 15 megaton yield was anything but small. Not only was it more powerful than the Mike test, it was 2.5 times larger than estimated. This meant that the original weight estimates for a low megaton class fusion device were too high. Confirmation

of this then came two months later with the successful test of the W-15 warhead on 14 May.

Though only weighing 7,600 pounds [139 inches long by 34.7 inches in diameter], the W-15 warhead produced a two megaton explosion. This was four times the yield of the W-18 bomb while being almost 3,000 pounds lighter. And even lighter bombs were on the drawing board. Bombs with megaton yields, but weighing only 2,000 pounds or less. Armed with these small bombs the B-64A Navaho could carry up to three warheads.[4]

New Competition

The development of small, high yield, thermonuclear devices did more than solve the Navaho's payload problem. It also changed the ICM playing field.

While Navaho and Snark had been receiving most of the Air Force's interest and money, the Atlas program had continued in the background. Though the Air Force increased funding in 1952, the major problem was the weight of the warhead. At 9,000 pounds plus, the available fission and fusion warheads were too heavy for a ballistic missile.

To put the problem in physical proportions, in 1953 Convair proposed a preliminary design for the Atlas missile. The vehicle was 90 feet tall, 12 feet wide and had five main engines producing 600, 000 pounds of thrust. The overall weight of this vehicle was well over 400,000 pounds or 200 tons. Greater in weight then the much later Titan II ICBM, this design was too large to be militarily practical.

With the success of the Bravo bomb, the ICBM situation changed rapidly. With these new payload figures, Convair reduced the size of the Atlas to 75 feet long and 10 feet wide.

Projected weight was around 260,000 pounds requiring only 360,000 pounds of thrust to achieve liftoff. This reduced figure could easily be accomplished by three engines.

Approving of the design changes, in December of 1954 the Air Force froze the Atlas design. On 14 January 1955, Convair was then issued a letter contract to develop and test their design. On that day Northrop Aircraft's Snark missile [MX-775] ceased to be the Navaho's prime competitor for the title of first U.S. Inter-Continental Missile.

The Big Split

With a new design, and new competition, the Navaho program had to undergo one more major change. In 1955 North American Aircraft decided that the Navaho program had grown too big for one division to handle. Thus, on 7 November NAA broke up the program into three separate divisions.

The first was the Missile Development Division [MDD]. Based at the old Consolidated Vultee plant at Downey California, this division would design, develop, and test new missile concepts. It also would serve as the final integration point for missile components.

The second division was the Autonetics division. Created from the electro-mechanical group at Downey, it moved into a new facility in Anaheim California. There it continued development of the N6A inertial guidance system, as well as avionics for other military programs.

The third and final division was Rocketdyne. Made from the propulsion division it moved into a new facility in Canoga Park, Los Angeles, California. Now closer to the test facility in Santa Susanna, it would continue development of the Navaho engine. It also would develop new engines for other applications and/or other missile programs.

Primarily, the breakup was done because the last two divisions were winning contracts separate from the Navaho program.[5] Rocketdyne was producing engines for both the Navaho and Redstone missile programs. It also was involved in the development of RATO systems for U.S. aircraft and, in early 1954, it had won the contract for the Atlas missile engine. Soon after the breakup it landed the development contracts for the Jupiter and Thor IRBMs engines.

As for Autonetics, it's work on autopilots and inertial guidance systems was landing it several new military contracts. It was developing the North American A-5 Vigilante's radar guidance and bombing system. It also was developing a special planar array search and ranging radar for the Convair F-106D and the F-86D.

WS-104A, Phase Three

The G-38

As stated earlier, the G-38 or XSM-64A was to be the final phase of the Navaho program. Development of the G-38 officially began with the start of preliminary system design in May of 1952. In October NAA completed this analysis, following which preliminary design of the G-38 booster began in December of 1952. Preliminary design of the G-38 missile then began in March of 1953.

A artist conception of a G-38 missile erect on its mobile launcher. This drawing is one of the best representations of what North American expected the G-38 to look like. This arrow Sleek missile would have been an interesting sight at military bases around the country. Photo By: Dale D. Meyer.

The next year would see big changes in the G-38 due to changes in its intended warhead. Breaking from the all ready in development XJ47-W-5 ramjets, in April preliminary design began on a still more powerful engine. Two months later NAA selected the 405,000 pound thrust engine for the G-38 booster [in design since August 1952].

With the engine selected, in September of 1954 construction began on the G-38 mockup. North American engineers then completed the preliminary design of the G-38 missile in December. Detailed design was underway by March of 1955 and in June the Air Force inspected the vehicle mockup.

Specifications [G-38]

Dimensions

Missile

Length:	87.3'	Span:	40.2'
Diameter:	6.5'	Weight:	120,500 lbs.

Booster

Length: 90 feet   Diameter: 7.8 '

Performance
Missile
    Speed: Mach 3.25   Ceiling: 71,000'
    Range:5,500 Nautical miles

Booster
    Altitude of engine burnout: 71,000'
    Altitude of vehicle separation: 71,000'

Propulsion:
    Missile: Two Wright Aeronautical RJ 47 ramjets.
        Maximum thrust: 20,070ibs.

    Booster: Three Rocketdyne LR83-NA-1 liquid fuel rocket
        engines
        Fuel Liquid Oxygen and Kerosene
        Maximum Thrust: 405,000 lbs

Guidance: N6B Inertial Navigation Unit with a PIX10
        Autopilot.

Payload: 10,000 obs. [15,000 lbs for reduced range]
        [capable of delivering three separate warheads]

The G-38 was exactly what North American had promised the Air Force. It could carry a large [5 ton] nuclear warhead a distance of 5,500 nautical miles. Cruise speed was Mach 3.25 and cruise altitude was 70,000 feet. No manned fighter or surface-to-air missile of the period could catch it. Finally, it was mobile and thus immune to a preemptive strike.

The vehicle was a highly sophisticated aerodynamic design for the period. Not only was the canard full flying, but the canards could work in tandem, unlike the G-26 and X-10. Instead of a rudder, the G-38's single vertical tail rotated. This system was a prelude to the rotating tail units of the later XB-70 Valkyrie bomber. Roll control was by full flying wing tip elevons. Only one other missile of the period used this type of control surface: the Bomarc.

The Avionics also were the most advanced available. A few years after the development of the transistor, the electronics of the G-38 were modular [etched] circuit boards. This use of solid state circuitry made the G-38's guidance and autopilot more reliable, durable and repairable than those of other missiles. The G-38 also pioneered the use of tape-programmed automatic checkout equipment.

The booster engines of the G-38 were by far one of the greatest advances. A three engine cluster producing over 400,000 pounds of thrust. Not until the first Titan II ICBM flew in March of 1962 did the United States have a booster with greater thrust. The three engines also were gimbaled, the first large rocket engine system to use this thrust vectoring method.

Finally, the Navaho's inertial guidance system was the most advanced unit available. Unlike the Atlas's radio control system, Navaho was immune to electronic [radio] jamming and EMP.[6] While the missile was in transit, the N6B autonavigator also was constantly determining the launcher's exact location.[7] This allowed the Navaho launch crew to fire the missile within 30 minutes of receiving a launch order anywhere in the United States.

The G-38's Dark Side.
Though the Navaho was a highly sophisticated and survivable missile system, it also was a logistics nightmare. Dimensionally, it was as large as the 1953 Atlas missile design: the rejected design. A Douglas C-133 transport, the largest cargo plane available, could not carry either the booster or the missile. Only after the development of the C-5 Galaxy in the late 60s was a vehicle large enough to carry this missile system. Thus, to move the Navaho long distances meant the use of trains, slowing its mobility.

Its great weight and bulk also would have made ground mobile operations difficult. Though a combined transport/erector launcher was in development, it would have required three lane highways for mobility. The system also would have required vehicles for the transport of the launch crew, fuel and spare parts. Included in this growing convoy was a troop of U.S. Air Force security personnel. Their job was to see that nothing happened to the missile during transit. Thus, to move one Navaho missile would snarl traffic for miles.

Finally, the G-38's wings were made of titanium, a rare and expensive metal. This metal was used because of the extreme temperatures [over 750 degrees F] the vehicle encountered at Mach 3.25. For a manned vehicle that was to be used many times, no one questioned the use of titanium. For a disposable vehicle like the Navaho however it made the missile extremely expensive.

All this was in comparison to the Atlas missile. Unlike the Navaho, a C-133 transport aircraft could carry this missile anywhere in North America. This made it easy to transport replacement or reload missiles to fixed launch sites scattered throughout the United States. The use of fixed launch sites, though vulnerable to attack, also made support and security for the Atlas significantly easier and cheaper.

Finally, the Mach 12 Atlas could deliver its warhead within thirty minutes of launch. The Mach 3 G-38 however took more than two hours to reach its target. It was this greater flight time that required the development of the N6 autonavigator. It also made the Navaho more vulnerable to interception by defensive missiles.[8]

This is not to say the Atlas was a perfect weapon system. Its radio control guidance was a liability and its thin – pressure stabilized – skin made the missile easy to damage. In truth its real virtue over the Navaho was its lower production and operation costs.

Opposite: This is the author's drawing of the G-38 based on information supplied by North American Engineers. The drawing is not accurate, given the canards are patterned after those on the G-26. The drawing however is an acceptable three view of the proposed vehicle. Photo By: Author.

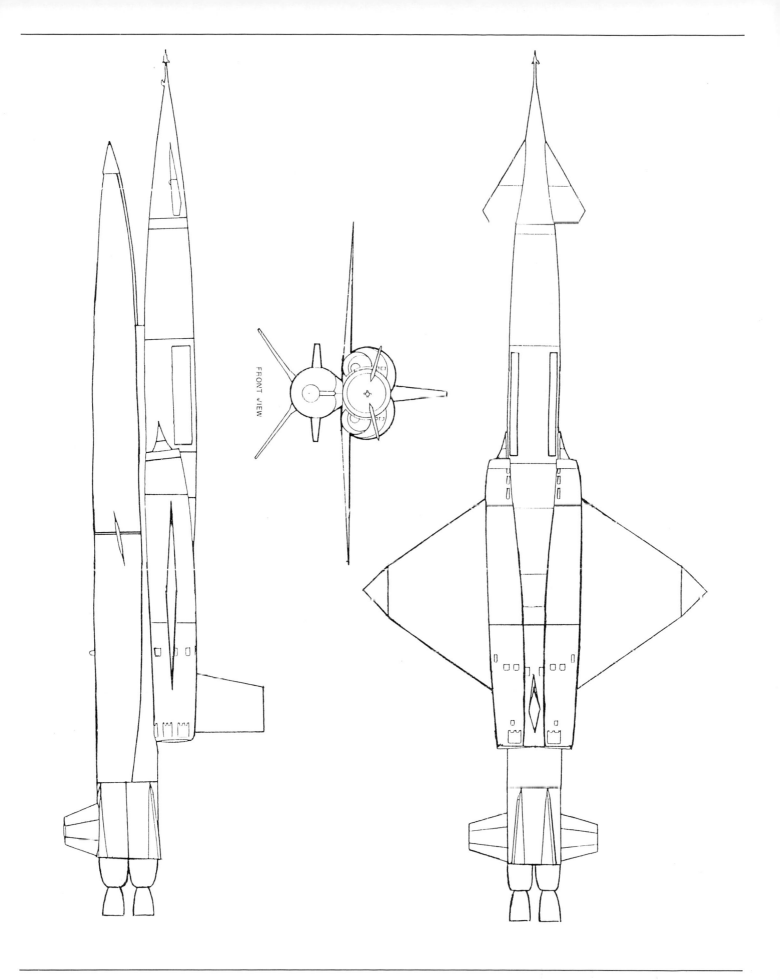

FRONT VIEW

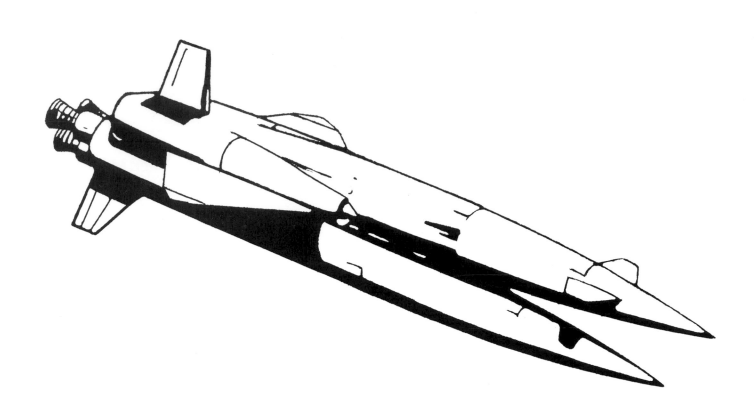

A drawing of the G-38 taken from a North American Chronology. This representation makes the vehicle look blunt and fat. In truth the missile was to have a higher fineness ratio (length verses cross sectional area) then the G-26. Photo By: NAA Chronology.

This was where the Navaho program stood in Mid-1955. One missile in testing, one in construction and the final design in development. The program had undergone significant changes, primarily due to changes in the world situation. North American Aviation also had changed, expanding to four divisions and employing more than ten thousand people in the Southern California area. Yet all this work rested on the success of the X-10 and G-26 flights at the Cape.

NOTES

(1) Monocoque structure is used throughout the aerospace industry. In this type of structure the skin of the vehicle carries most – if not all – of the structural load.

(2) A problem with the Mk-4 and other early fission warheads was the requirement that the fuel capsule remain separate until just before the bomb was dropped. On a manned aircraft a specially trained crew member inserted the capsule before release. On a missile, an automated device called an In-Flight Inserter [IFI] was required. It also required that the payload section be large enough to contain both the bomb, the fuel capsule and the insertion unit in separate areas. This significantly complicated the Navaho design as well as reduced its reliability.

(3) The Air Force never operationally deployed the Super ORalloy bomb. Sources state the device carried such a massive amount of fissionable material that aluminum chains were inserted to prevent

a premature chain reaction. These chains were pulled out when the bomb was dropped. Such an extraction system was not possible for the Navaho.

(4) A North American paper dated in late 1959 states the G-38 could carry multiple warheads. To do this however would have required significant changes in the Navaho missile. Engineers would have had to add a bomb bay door, and upgrade the structure to take the strain of opening the bay at Mach 3. The vehicle also would have had to have a method of pressurizing the bomb bay between drops.

(5) The North American Aircraft Division at El Segundo, the original site of the Navaho program, also was gaining new contracts. In 1955 it landed the X-15 rocket plane project, the F-108 Mach three interceptor and the XB-70 Mach three bomber program. Though not Navaho related, these programs would benefit from Navaho research.

(6) EMP stands for Electro-Magnetic Pulse. All nuclear detonations produce EMP to one degree or another. If a nuclear warhead was detonated in the atmosphere over an Atlas site, the pulse would temporarily scramble the radio control system. Surprisingly, it also would temporarily make the Navaho's modular [transistorized] electronics inoperable.

(7) To program a missile you need two pieces of information: target location and launch site location. The more accurately you know the launch site's position relative to the target, the more accurate the missile will be. Having an INU as accurate as the N6 is useless if the data used to program it is inaccurate.

(8) Both missiles eventually became vulnerable to interception. Anti-ballistic missiles like the Nike Zeus or Sprint could intercept both with relative ease. To counter such systems modern ICBMs carry radar jamming chaff and decoy warheads. The Navaho also could have carried chaff and ECM systems like modern manned bombers.

Chapter 4

Cape Testing

The Cape, 1955

The move to Cape Canaveral Auxiliary Air Force Base [CCAAFB] had been a part of the Navaho program from the very beginning. The Air Force Missile test Center [AFMTC] was the only place that allowed straight-line flights of over 1,500 miles without passing over populated areas. This improved both public safety and military security, an important issue since the Navaho was "Top Secret." AFMTC also was one of the most isolated areas of the country.

To the east of Cape Canaveral is the Atlantic Ocean. This area was monitored by small patrol boats and large B-17s. On the west side of the Cape was the Banana River, a large shallow zone which made undetected approach difficult. As for the other compass headings: swamps, alligators, water moccasins and rattle snakes made unauthorized observers rare.

Where the AFMTC offered significant advantages over Edwards, it also had its problems. The most obvious was the Skid Strip the X-10s would use for landings. Begun in July of 1953, it had the same dimensions as the simulation at Edwards AFB [300' X 10,000']. The major difference however was that if an X-10 over ran the runway at Edwards, it just kept going onto the dry, hard packed, lake bed. At the AFMTC, if an X-10 overran the Skid Strip it landed in an area of soft sand.

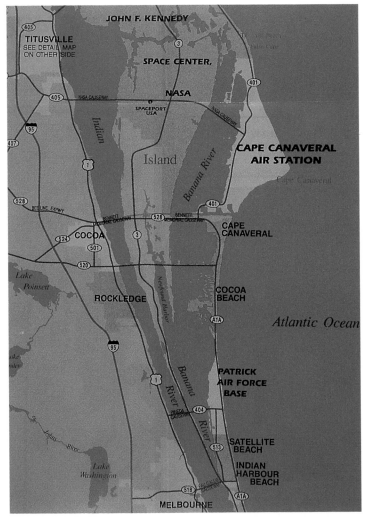

A color map of the Cape Canaveral area. The Cape Canaveral Auxiliary Air Force Station is a very isolated facility. Originally, access was only possible via a narrow strip of land running up from Patrick AFB. When America began developing missiles, it became the perfect place to test the weapons in secret. Photo by: U.S. Air Force, Cape Canaveral AFB.

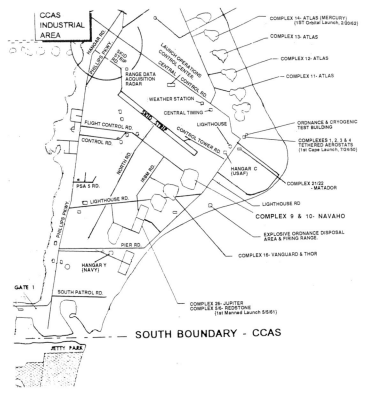

A map of the Cape Canaveral Air Station showing the location of the Skid Strip and the Navaho launch complexes 9 and 10. Also shown are some of the missile launch sites being constructed or used during the Navaho test period. Missing from this is the Snark test site, though it was just north of the lighthouse. Photo by: U.S. Air Force, Cape Canaveral AFB.

North American opened its field office at Patrick AFB in the Spring of 1953. Originally operations were to have begun in July of 1953 but construction delays made this impossible. It was not until mid-1953 that the Air Force issued construction contracts for the two Missile Assembly Buildings with supporting utilities. Also issued then were construction contracts for the Flight Control Building and Guidance Laboratory number two. Construction of the first G-26 launch site, Vertical Launch Facility No.1 [Complex 9], then began in September. These delays were only the beginning.

By the Spring of 1954 the Air Force had rescheduled the initial occupation date for the Flight Control Building to February 1955. Construction of the missile assembly building also was behind schedule, its new completion date was March 1955. Range Safety officials also were having difficulty extending the range to 1,500 miles to accommodate the G-26 vehicle. This extension would require the building of tracking and control facilities off Haiti and Antigua.

Regardless of the construction delays, conditional occupancy of the guidance laboratory began in the fall of 1954. In January 1955 the Air Force also allowed North American engineers conditional occupancy of the launch pad, blockhouse, and Flight Control Building. This was not because the buildings were completed, but because the first X-10 flight was only six months off. Installation of last minute equipment would continued until February.

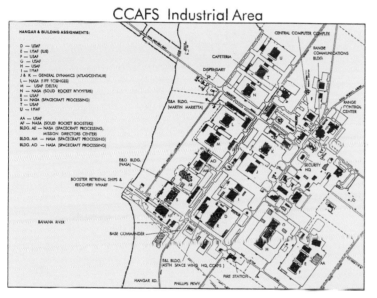

CCAFS Industrial Area

The Cape Canaveral Air Station Industrial Area. This is where all the work is really done. Here are the hangers, missile assembly buildings, and laboratories. The Navaho program used buildings E and F according to Cape records. Unfortunately, the building numbering sequence may have changed in forty years. The only place that has not changed is the cafeteria where everyone ate. Photo by: U.S. Air Force, Cape Canaveral AFB.

In March Missile Assembly Hangar "F" was completed, and launch complex 9 began operational checkout. The first X-10 [GM-19312] and the QF-80 drone fighter also arrived that month. The QF-80 would test the automatic landing system at AFMTC, and perform simulated X-10 flights for the range tracking system.

In April the Air Force turned over Building "E" to North American. That same month the Air Force also began considering the procurement of a barrier system for the Skid Strip. This device would stop the X-10 if the missile's parabrake did

not open.[1] The plan was approved in May and by July the barrier system was completed.

The barrier was a unique feature of the Cape test flights. The system was usually placed at the 7,500 foot mark down the Skid-Strip. Activation was by the nose wheel of the X-10 rolling over a trigger line. This would release a set of arms that would spring up along the side of the Skid-Strip. Suspended between these arms was a heavy metal cable that would catch the X-10's main gear.

Attached to either end of the cable was a long anchor chain. This chain stretched down the side of the runway from the 7,500 foot mark to the end of the Skid-Strip. As the main gear pulled the cable forward off the arms, the X-10 began dragging the chain onto the runway. With each link of chain the X-10 pulled onto the runway, the vehicle began dragging more and more weight. This system could stop an X-10 in less than 1,000 feet if properly engaged.

A close-up of the left main gear strut of X-10 number one [19307] at Wright Patterson AFB Museum. The barrier cable would catch the gear strut at mid-length. The strut was not very strong, and was not designed to withstand the moment loads the barrier creates. Yet when the barrier functioned the strut held, even in one case where the barrier only caught one strut. Photo by: Author.

With the arrival of the first X-10 finally the Air Force began considering ways of improving the range tracking system. At that time the range used optical cameras to monitor/track test missiles. This system was effective for subsonic and low altitude missiles, but a high altitude Mach 2 vehicle like the X-10 stretched its limits. Furthermore, the system failed during periods of low clouds forcing the range to shutdown because of weather.

In July of 1955 AFMTC personnel attended a meeting at Redstone Arsenal to discuss the acquisition of Nike Ajax type radars for the Cape. The plan was to deploy three modified AN/MPQ-26 units at three stations along the test range. The Army approved of this plan and set 1 October 1955 as the target date for delivery of the units. Initial Operational Capability was to be on 1 April 1956 in time for the first G-26 tests.

The Neighbors
Where the area surrounding the Air Force Missile Test Center was sparsely populated, the center itself was teaming with people. Within this controlled area several companies were testing missile designs for both the Air Force and the Army.

An early Bomarc A sits on a launcher at Patrick AFB Though never fired from the Cape, the Bomarcs were tested at the Air Force Missile Test Center. The missile in this picture [Number 13] is having its control surfaces cycled prior to a launch. Many years later the Bomarc and Navaho programs would combine in the short lived X-10 Drone program. Photo by: U.S. Air Force.

A Matador launch from the Cape, 18 July 1951. This is an early Matador of the mid-wing design, all production missiles were high wing. Note the Cape lighthouse in the background. As the earlier maps indicate, the Matador launch facility was just north of the lighthouse. The Matador launch facility also fired its missiles due south, not south-east as the range is laid out. The missiles had to make a left turn soon after launch to align with the range. Photo by: U.S. Air Force, Patrick AFB.

In one section of CCAAFB was the Air Force Matador training facility. After years of development, missile MX-771 was now in service with the Air Force. By 1954 two squadrons were in Western Germany [one hundred nuclear armed missiles]. Before the start of X-10 testing, the Matador program was the principal user of the AFMTC range.

In another section, Boeing and Westinghouse engineers were working on the Bomarc surface-to-air missile system. An outgrowth of the Air Forces GARPA program, Bomarc was an unmanned interceptor aircraft. Eventually, it could intercept supersonic bombers or cruise missiles like the X-10.

The United States Army also was at the Cape launching Redstone missiles. The Redstones were famous at the Cape for their punctuality compared to the other missile systems. Matador missiles were notorious for canceling a scheduled launch date at launch time. In the Navaho program, the first X-10 flight was canceled three times for various reasons. And for hold times a Bomarc missile was held for a record 20.2 hours before it was launched. The Redstones however were so consistent that base personnel set their watches by their launch.

In 1956 a Redstone did not launch as scheduled. Though unusual, a few days later the same missile failed again to leave its pad. The next day several VIPs, including Werner von Braun came down from Redstone Arsenal, Alabama to see what was wrong.

This incident was significant in that the missile had recently entered service. It is possible that the launch team for this missile was the first Army unit to begin training with the Redstone. Whatever the problem was however, the third attempt proved successful and the Redstone program returned to normal.

A Redstone tanks up on LOX prior to a launch. The super cold liquid has chilled the missile's skin causing water to condense and freeze around it. The Redstones were the most reliable rocket in testing at AFMTC in 1956. Its Navaho developed engine made it the longest range missile in the free world. Photo by: U.S. Army.

Of course, the most important group present at AFMTC was Convair's WS-107A team [Project Atlas]. In December of 1954 the Air Force selected the North Beach area of Cape Canaveral as the location for the Atlas launch facilities. Construction was swift and by the time the first X-10 flew at the Cape, two launching pads for X-17 rockets were in service. Flight tests of proposed re-entry vehicles then began on the X-17s in July.

The Snark

One of the largest teams at AFMTC was NAAs old rival Northrop. For three years Northrop had been launching test vehicles at AFMTC as part of its MX-775 Snark program. Though rapidly being outpaced by newer systems, this missile was still in the running for the title "The First U.S. Intercontinental Missile."

The Snark

SPECIFICATIONS (N-69E)

Length: 69'	Span: 42'
Height: 15'	Weight: 51,000 lbs

An early Atlas A sits on its launch pad at the Cape. This early test vehicle has a fake re-entry vehicle [RV] and no sustainer engine. Its range was less than that of a IRBM and it was radio controlled. Yet it was the primary competitor to the Navaho thanks to its Navaho developed rocket engines. Photo by: U.S. Air Force.

PERFORMANCE

Speed: Mach 0.94   Ceiling: over 60,000'
Range: 6,300 miles

PROPULSION:

Sustainer - One 11,500 pound thrust Pratt & Whitney J57-P-17 Turbojet engine
Booster - Two 130,000 pound thrust Allegheny Ballistics solid fuel rocket motors

GUIDANCE: Inertial system with star tracker

WARHEAD: Operationally deployed with one W-39 thermo nuclear warhead of 4 megaton yield
NOS. MISSILES: 30 known deployed,

Northrop's Snark program shows how two different companies can meet the same military requirement in different

An N-69 Snark sits in its hanger at the Cape. The tracked tug and tow bar shows the vehicle is being readied for transfer to the launch site. The tracked tug makes you wonder if the road to the launch site was not yet paved Photo by: Northrop Aircraft.

ways. This missile was to extend the potential of a subsonic ground launched cruise missile beyond the capabilities of the then in service Matador missile. Only a radical aircraft designer as John Northrop could have produced a functional vehicle design using low risk technology [fully developed].

Like so many of Northrop's designs, the Snark was a tailless missile. This gave the vehicle both low aerodynamic drag and a low radar image. To control pitch without a tail, the Snark used special wing elevons. These elevons also controlled roll and to some degree yaw, though a rudder also was present. In good weather the vehicle's autopilot regularly produced stable flight. In high turbulence however the missile usually broke up.

Like the Navaho, the Snark had undergone several changes since the program began in 1946. Originally called the N-25, it was to deliver a Mk-5 fission bomb a distance of 5,500 miles. In 1952 however Northrop enlarged the design to carry a 10,000 pound hydrogen bomb. Now called the N-

69, this test vehicle had been at the AFMTC since late 1953. By the time the X-10s began flights testing at the Cape, 18 Snarks had been tested. None of these missiles completed their flights however, four did not even survive for one minute of flight.

An interesting fact of the Snark program was that in 1954 Northrop considered using a North American guidance unit. On 12 November 1954 an N-69B Snark carried a North American guidance unit. The flight was mostly successful, but on landing approach the missile suddenly stalled following landing skid extension. This device was possibly the XN-2B Stellar Inertial Unit tested in 1952.

In a later test on 13 January 1955 a Snark flew with a data recorder identified as an N-2C. This might have been a variant of the NAA N-2 system or a unit developed by Northrop.

By 1955 Northrop occupied as much of the Cape as North American Aviation. It had two missile assembly hangers, support facilities, a three launcher site with bunker, and Guid-

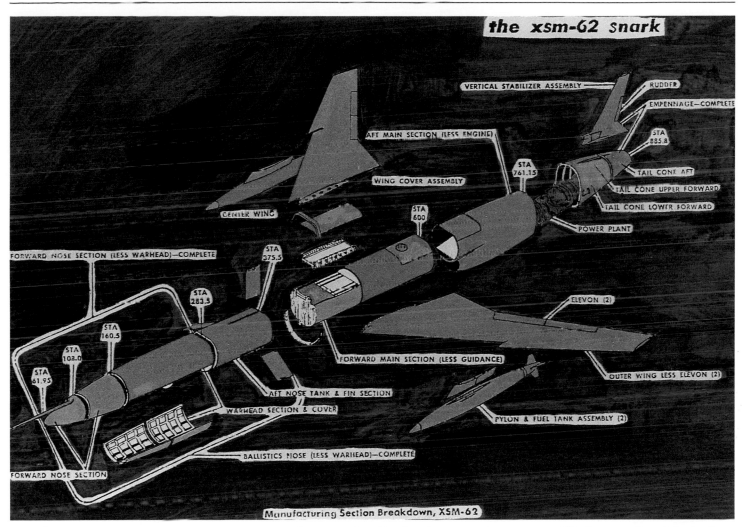

AFT MAIN SECTION (LESS ENGINE)

VERTICAL STABILIZER ASSEMBLY — RUDDER

EMPENNAGE—COMPLETE

STA 885.8

TAIL CONE AFT

TAIL CONE UPPER FORWARD

TAIL CONE LOWER FORWARD

POWER PLANT

STA 761.15

WING COVER ASSEMBLY

STA 600

CENTER WING

FORWARD NOSE SECTION (LESS WARHEAD)—COMPLETE

STA 375.5

STA 283.5

STA 160.5

STA 108.0

STA 61.95

STA 61.95

ELEVON (2)

FORWARD MAIN SECTION (LESS GUIDANCE)

OUTER WING LESS ELEVON (2)

AFT NOSE TANK & FIN SECTION

WARHEAD SECTION & COVER

PYLON & FUEL TANK ASSEMBLY (2)

BALLISTICS NOSE (LESS WARHEAD)—COMPLETE

FORWARD NOSE SECTION

Manufacturing Section Breakdown, XSM-62

An exploded view of the Snark showing its key subassemblies. The Snark was the low cost, no frills intercontinental missile. Using already developed technology, it was the only design that was expected to work in 1956. Within two years it also was completely obsolete. Photo by: Author.

ance Laboratory number one. By July of 1956 the Ascension Island station was to have the minimum instrumentation necessary to monitor the impact of production Snark missiles. This was a little ahead of schedule considering that it would not be until late 1957 before the first Snark reached the island.[2]

Northrop's lack of success with the early Snark vehicles prompted a joke by North Americans engineers. The statement was that the state of Florida should post warning signs reading "Danger, Snark Infested Waters." Within a year the Northrop engineers would have a far meaner statement for the Navaho program.

The ICM Race

At this point you may have realized that in mid-1955 there were three companies at the Cape developing an Intercontinental Missile [ICM]. Convair's Atlas, thanks to Rocketdyne engines and small hydrogen bombs was rapidly becoming the primary program. It was to be the ultimate weapon: immune to interception, fast, and destructive.

The only problem with the Atlas was that it was a paper missile. Convair's engineers had only launched three mis-

The Snark launch site at the Cape. From this picture the Snark site appears to have been just north of the lighthouse just off Central Control Road. In this picture you can see the blockhouse and three fixed launchers. A portable cover is also in the picture. This cover gave launch technicians some cover against sudden Florida rain storms.

siles, all technical failures and all before 1950. Rocketdyne was still testing the engines and construction of the first vehicle frame had only begun. Anything could still go wrong with this program.

A production Snark [SM-65] sits on a production mobile launcher at the Cape. This U.S. ICM was the first to actually achieve intercontinental range. It also was obsolete before it was ready for service. Technology was advancing so quickly most of the missiles deployed in the mid-to-late 1950s were obsolete before they were operational. And those that were not obsolete when deployed became that way in a scant few years. Photo by: Northrop Aircraft.

Northrop on the other hand was already testing its pre-production prototype missile. Though none of the 17 flights completed were successful, a few were partial. In four flights the vehicle completed its flight only to crash during landing. In another flight, the failure was caused by the missile colliding with its chase plane.

In the middle was North American who only had its X-10s in flight testing. Its rocket technology was well developed, and its N-6 autonavigation unit had flown on a Convair T-29 transport, but the G-26 missile was still in static testing. Flight testing of this missile would not begin until May 1956, with the first G-38 not flying until 1959.

In the end the Air Force continued all three programs to insure the deployment of an ICM in the shortest possible time. On 23 September 1955 the Air Force issued North American the design, fabrication and test contract for the G-38. In all the Air Force ordered nine G-38 missiles, 12 boosters and 21 N6B autonavigation units. The next month X-10 testing began at the Cape.

The Nation's Race
The race to develop an intercontinental missile was more than an industry race. By 1956 the United States government was aware that the Soviet Union was developing medium and intermediate range ballistic missiles. With this knowledge the old fear of a Russian nuclear tipped Intercontinental Missile returned.

This was the beginning of the period many historians now call "The Missile Gap." A period when the United States had little concrete information on Soviet missile capabilities. As a result, the government worked to deploy as many nuclear missiles as possible. A superb example of this drive to deploy nuclear systems was the development of the Thor IRBM.

Of all the missiles developed at this time, the Thor Is the best example of the mid-1950s drive to deploy strategic nuclear missiles. In a scant three years this missile went from Air Force requirement to the testing of production vehicles. Everything from its engine, guidance, RV and even structure was taken from other missile programs to cut development time. Without the work done on the Navaho and Atlas programs, this missile would never have flown in 1957. Photo by: McDonnell-Douglas.

The Air Force issued a General Operational Requirement for an IRBM on 2 December 1954. By late August of 1955 the Air Force Ballistic Missile division had already determined the Thor's dimensions [set to a C-124 cargo bay]. The engine was to be a variant of the Atlas booster engine, and the re-entry vehicle was the Atlas Mk-2. The guidance system also was from the Atlas program.

After receiving the contract on 23 December 1955, Douglas completed the Thor's design in eight months. No prototypes were built allowing production to begin in August of 1956. Douglas delivered the first vehicle on 26 October 1956, less than two years after the Air Force issued the GOR.

Testing Begins
It had taken three years but North American was ready to begin testing at Cape Canaveral Auxiliary Air Force Base.

The first X-10s had arrived, the Skid-Strip was ready and the G-26 launcher had been tested. The time had come for North American to begin flying its design.

The following text is a time line of North American Cape activities over the next two years. Instead of separating the testing of the X-10 and later G-26, they have been combined in their proper historical sequence. Important events also have been included at their proper place in the time line. This gives you a true feel for the program, its victories and its defeats.

X-10 Flight 16

The first X-10 flight at the Cape was on 19 August 1955. The vehicle was number six [GM-19312], the last of the Edwards number series. Its mission was to test vehicle stability and control and vehicle body bending characteristics. It also was to be the first X-10 to land at the Cape using the closed loop approach and auto landing system.

Number six flew its mission well, performing both the stability and the body bending tests. During its landing however the parabrake did not deploy. The emergency barrier system

An X-10 drone comes in for a landing at the Cape. This vehicle is reported to have been GM52-5 during a flight in 1958. It is shown here simply because this is as far as X-10 GM19312 and GM52-4 got: landing. Like this vehicle would in 1958, these X-10s completed their flight only to fall victim of the skid strip during landing. Photo by: U.S. Air Force, Patrick AFB.

malfunctioned and the missile ran off the end of the runway into the soft sand.

The nose wheel sank almost immediately on reaching the sandy area. The X-10 however, was still moving forward under its own momentum. The moment force this produced on the nose wheel strut was greater then the support bulkhead could handle. The result was the failure of this bulkhead and the rupturing of the number two fuel tank which the bulkhead was the front end of. The remaining jet fuel in the tank spilled out and then ignited destroying the missile by fire.

X-10 Flight 17

The second X-10 flight at the Cape was on 24 October 1955. The X-10 used in this flight was number 11 [GM 52-4], the first of the Cape series of missiles.

The original mission of vehicle eleven was to prove the X-10's structural integrity during a dive-in. With the loss of vehicle six, and because it was instrumented for structural tests, NAA changed the mission to testing vehicle control, stability and body bending. The structural integrity dive-in flight could then be performed later.

A problem with the X-10's J40 engines prevented the missile from completing its mission. After a few low speed maneuvers to test stability and control, ground control then guided number 11 back to the Cape. Once there, bad weather forced the cancellation of the steep angle closed-loop approach and auto landing. A normal ground control landing was then used.

The normal angle auto approach and landing of number 11 was successful. After rolling some 1,000 feet down the Skid-Strip however, the shimmy damper on the nose wheel failed. Now uncontrollable, X-10 number 11 drifted off the edge of the runway. After rolling an additional 3,000 feet on the runway edge, it then hit a section of soft sand. The nose wheel failed, rupturing the number two fuel tank. A fire then broke out in the nose wheel well, destroying the vehicle.

The loss of missiles six and 11 produced a major delay in the X-10 program. Testing of this missile would not resume until North American personnel finished re-assembling the third Cape X-10, vehicle number eight. During this delay however, in December NAA completed three successful static firings of a prototype booster at Complex 9. A fourth and final firing of 31 second duration then occurred on 6 January 1956. These tests completed the checkout of the Navaho program's fixed G-26 launcher. The booster was then airlifted back to North American's Downey facility for post test inspection.

While the booster tests were going on, in January of 1956 the Air Force announced a major realignment of the Navaho program. The new plan was to have the G-38 in service by October 1960, two years early. To do this the Air Force would reduce the number of planned G-38 test flights from 84 to 40. The number of training and suitability flights was also reduced from 20 to 10. These changes in the G-38 phase of the Navaho program would have major implications to the G-26 program.

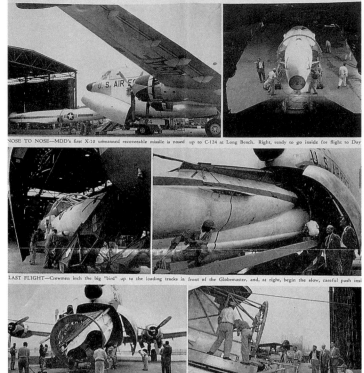

'OLD NO. 1' FLIES IN STATE TO ITS FINAL PLACE OF HONO

NOSE TO NOSE—MDD's first X-10 unmanned recoverable missile is nosed up to C-124 at Long Beach. Right, ready to go inside for flight to Day

LAST FLIGHT—Crewmen inch the big "bird" up to the loading tracks in front of the Globemaster, and, at right, begin the slow, careful push insi

BIG BITE—Looking as if it makes a nice mouthful for the C-124, the X-10 enters fuselage on an angle. Finally it is ready for trip to USAF Museu

X-10 Moves to USAF Museum Display . . .

(Continued from Page 1, Column 5) failed to extend and the missile was brought in for a belly landing on Muroc Dry Lake at Edwards AFB.

However, automatic approach and landing was accomplished with very little structural damage, so the nightmare of a wheels-up landing turned out to be little more than a disturbing dream. Three months later No. 1 was back in the air.

Another high point in its ca-

Globemaster from Long Beach to Dayton. There it will be put on permanent display outside the Air Force Museum alongside the X-3 experimental airplane.

Symbols of Flights

On the aft section of the port engine nacelle you can read its history as depicted by an MDD artist. A separate "bird" symbol for each flight tells the story. Over the first bird is a question mark, indicative of a bit of skept-

Joe Pomykata, first X-10 project engineer, and Herb Langmore, his successor, explain as exclamations that it did so well the second time. The third bird has a halo overhead—it was a troublesome flight and no one thought No. 1 would get back. Off the nose of the fourth flight bird is a shockwave indicating it cracked the sound barrier and went supersonic.

Each succeeding flight symbol indicates a successful automatic

A sequence of images taken from a North American newsletter showing the loading of X-10 number one into a C-124 transport. The Edwards X-10s were trucked to the lake bed: producing some interesting stories. The Cape missiles were flown by transport to Patrick AFB. Because of the vehicle's design and the C-142's cargo bay dimensions, a special moving cradle was developed. This cradle rotated the missile along its X-axis so that it would clear certain cargo bay protrusions. Photo by: William F. Gibson Jr.

X-10 Flight 18

On 3 February 1956 North American rolled X-10 number eight [GM 52-1] out onto the Skid-Strip. The primary goal of the flight was to study vehicle aerodynamics at speeds up to Mach 2. A secondary role was to prove the Cape automatic landing system by successfully recovering the vehicle.

X-10 number eight took off perfectly and flew out over the Atlantic. Just past Station 3 [Grand Bahama Island], at an altitude of 47,000 feet, ground control turned it back towards the Cape. Maximum afterburner was then engaged and the vehicle began accelerating. By the time it was approaching the Cape it was traveling at Mach 1.9. The afterburners were then shutdown for range safety reasons.

X-10 number eight had one last test to perform on this flight, successful landing. The automatic approach system [Hero Scope] performed properly and the vehicle touched down 3,000 feet down the Skid-Strip. Control during the de-

GM 52-1 sits on the skid strip after a successful flight. NAA personnel are busy safeing the missile: this includes the removal of the destruct unit. The lack of a barrier cable indicates that this was probably its second flight on 29 February or the high angle approach on 20 March. The author believes it was the first given the signs of high temperature heating on the vehicle's paint Photo by: U.S. Air Force, Patrick AFB.

A G-26 bleeds off lox vapor at complex nine. During a similar operation the valve on the lox tank froze shut. As the pressure built-up, a Cape Range safety officer came up with a novel solution: a 30 caliber rifle! The pad engineers talked him out of perforating the missile and the valve subsequently opened of its own accord. Photo by: William F. Gibson Jr.

celeration roll was excellent even after deployment of the parabrake. The parabrake did not deploy fully however and at the 7,500 foot mark the vehicle contacted the barrier.

The barrier cable did not catch the left main gear. This made the barrier's braking effect non-uniform causing the vehicle to drift to the right side of the runway. Luckily, the vehicle received only minor damage. Total duration of the flight was 51 minutes and the vehicle flew 425 nautical miles.

Following number eight's flight, on 20 February Major William F Sandusky AFMTC attended a conference at the Wright Air Development Center, Wright AFB, Ohio. At this conference North American Aviation submitted a proposal titled "Project BROOMSTICK." In this proposal NAA would begin G-26 dive-in flights in 1956, one year ahead of schedule. This would allow the start of G-38 flights in June 1958 followed by deployment in 1960.

Broomstick called for the launching of four autonavigator equipped G-26 missiles with the first launch in October of 1956. These missiles would not only test the N-6A autonavigator, but also the missile's structural strength during dive-in. The impact area was to be St Lucia Island, south of Station 10 [Antigua Island].

In addition to the autonavigator, the Broomstick missiles differed from the standard G-26 in the absence of landing gear. Since the missile's were to dive in on their target, they did not need recovery equipment like landing gear or parachutes. The removal of these items reduced vehicle flight weight, increasing the maximum range.

With the Broomstick missiles, North American also planned to fly seven G-26 radio controlled aerodynamic test missiles. Launched alternately with the Broomstick missiles, these G-26s would test the vehicle's aerodynamics, structure, and control system. In the first six flights, the missiles would fly to Station 5 [San Salvador Island] and then back to the Cape for recovery. The seventh flight however would fly to San Salvador and then back to Station 3 [Grand Bahama Island] for a dive in test.

This alternating launch system may seem strange but it was very important in this accelerated program. The first G-26 flight was to be an aerodynamic missile to prove out the airframe. The next flight, a broomstick missile, would then prove the auto-navigator and the dive-in attack method. If this flight failed, an aerodynamic test vehicle would follow to determine the problem. If the Broomstick flight was successful, the second aerodynamic flight would then test the mobile launcher.

X-10 Flight 19

On 29 February 1956 a second flight was completed with X-10 number eight [GM 52-1]. Like the previous mission, this flight was to study the vehicle's high speed performance. This time the missile was to exceed Mach 2.

The speed run began some 50 miles north of Station 4 [Eleuthera Island, Bahamas] at an altitude of 47,000 feet. It was still accelerating when it approached the Cape at Mach 2.1. Range Safety officers then ordered the test ended to prevent the vehicle from leaving the range area.

Number eight [GM52-1] just after landing on the skid strip. The air brakes are fully extended around the engine exhaust nozzles and the parabrake is fully deployed. This picture could have been of the flight on the 29th of February or on 20 March. Note the fire concern shown by the two fire engines. Photo by: U.S. Air Force, Patrick AFB.

This was the last recognized X-10 high speed flight. The remaining flights tested the G-26 landing system, the autonavigator or the dive-in attack method. Thus, we will never know the vehicle's maximum level flight speed. In concilia-

No this is not a colorized picture, this is how G-26 number one looked on the pad prior to its launch. The bright red orange color was to aid in tracking the vehicle at altitude. Surprisingly, at certain angles, the orange was so bright it shows up as white in B/W photos. The erection tower has been retracted and the vehicle seems ready for launch. Photo by: National Archives.

tion, this flight made X-10 number eight the fastest winged vehicle at the Cape in 1956.

After its record breaking speed run, number eight successfully landed using the automatic landing system. On landing approach the vehicle nearly undershot the Skid-Strip with touchdown occurring at the 225 foot mark. The vehicle then rolled some 4,000 feet before stopping, its nose wheel just 60 feet to the right of the center line. Total time for the flight was 62 minutes with a distance traveled of 547 miles.

X-10 Flight 20

The third flight of number eight occurred on 20 March 1956. The mission was to test the G-26 missile's high angle approach and recovery system.

Takeoff was uneventful with the X-10 flying out 80 miles before being turned around for its test landing. Maximum altitude was 26,000 feet and the speed was 250 knots [287 MPH]. When it arrived back at the Cape, it then performed the high angle landing maneuver.

The automatic landing was by all standards flawless. Touchdown was just 1,550 feet down the Skid Strip and only 15 feet to the left of the center line. Vehicle roll was a scant 3,500 feet leaving a good 2,000 feet left before the barrier [at the 7,500 ft mark].

The high approach angle of the G-26 is why the G-26 and the X-10 had twin tails. During this maneuver, a single vertical tail could be "Blanked Out" by the vehicle's body. This would cause a loss of rudder control, allowing the vehicle to drift off the runway. As for the planned G-38 missile, because it was not recoverable it would use a single, small, vertical tail. This produced less drag increasing missile range.

Six days after this X-10 flight, the first G-26 flight ready booster [No.003] arrived at the Cape. G-26 missile number one [GM10989] then followed in the first week of April. The first of the seven aerodynamic test missiles, assembly began immediately with a launch date for late May.

X-10 Flight 21

The sixth Cape flight occurred on 24 April 1956. This flight involved X-10 number nine [GM 52-2] a vehicle not originally planned for the Cape test flights. It would instead replace vehicle 11 [GM 52-4] which was to test vehicle structural integrity during dive-in.

The takeoff was normal but within 16 minutes the ground control system failed. At this point the vehicle was 120 miles out to sea, 32,000 feet up and traveling at Mach 1.4. Four minutes later the vehicle crashed into the water 27 miles south east of Grand Bahama Island.

The loss of control made the flight a technical failure. Tracking equipment at Station 3 [Grand Bahama Island] however showed that the vehicle stayed together until impact. Its impact speed was 825 knots [950 MPH] or Mach 1.25.

The failure of X-10 flight number 21 was compounded by problems with G-26 number one [GM10989]. The Auxiliary Power Unit arrived behind schedule and mechanically defective. Modifications and repairs postponed the first launch until July 1956.

Here is an example of what the author was talking about. Here is number one on complex 9, erecting tower in place. The missile looks almost completely white with the exception of some dark blotches on the wing. The missile however is actually white and bright orange red. Note the cover on the right side of the picture. This cover was placed over the missile when its was down to protect it and engineers from the weather. It was not of much help however for water seemed to get into everything on the G-26. Closed electrical couplings were found to have water in them, or worse green slime. Photo by: William F. Gibson Jr.

An unidentified G-26 sits on complex 9. This maybe number one, unfortunately the booster number is too hard to read. Note the light LOX bleed showing that the booster is fully filled with oxidizer. The number of men on the pad however shows that either a booster test or a launch is "NOT" pending. Photo by: William F. Gibson Jr.

X-10 GM52-5 [number 12] sits on the Skid strip being readied for flight. The colors on this missile were also used by GM-52-1: bright orange-red with white strips and a blue engine area. Unlike the Edwards X-10s most of the X-10s flown at the Cape during the Navaho program used these colors. Only GM19312 is reported to have been an Edwards white. Photo by: William F. Gibson Jr.

X-10 Flight 22

The seventh Cape flight was on 5 June 1956. The missile used was vehicle number 12 [GM 52-5]. Its mission was to test autonavigator control of the X-10. It also was to investigate the effects of environment on the navigation systems functions and accuracy.

Takeoff was normal and the vehicle headed out to sea for a subsonic test. Soon after however a computer malfunction occurred preventing the INUs guidance signals from reaching the autopilot. Ground control took over and the vehicle was flown some 280 nautical miles down range and then back to the Cape. Maximum speed was Mach 0.9 at an altitude of 35,000 feet.

On return the missile landed successfully using the auto approach and landing system. The parabrake did not fully deploy, but the barrier engaged properly. Some superficial fairing damage occurred due to the barrier, but otherwise the vehicle was unharmed.

The same month this X-10 flew the G-38 booster engine was first static fired at the Rocketdyne facility at Santa Susanna. This engine produced 405,000 pounds of thrust for 45.5 seconds. This was greater than that of the Atlas cluster which only produced 360,000 pounds of thrust.

In June the Air Force accepted the last X-10, vehicle number 13. With its delivery construction of the X-10 test missile ended at Downey. In July it arrived at the Cape for use in the autonavigator portion of the X-10 flight test program.

The arrival of X-10 number 13 would be marred by continuing problems with the G-26. Three different APUs had arrived, but none met flight requirements. While engineers worked to solve this problem, checks of the G-26 missile and the launch facility were conducted. By the original July launch date everything was ready except the APU.

X-10 Flight 23

On 18 July 1956 X-10 number 12 was set for a second attempt to test the N-6 autonavigator. This time it was at chock release where the computer system failed. Again only a partial evaluation could be made of the N-6 through an analysis of the telemetry. Control reverted to the radio control system and the X-10 was successfully landed back at the Cape.

The reason for the failure of these two X-10 flights is the source of some disagreement. One reason comes from a half year report filed at Patrick AFB for July/December 1956. According to this report the fault was a carbon pile voltage regulator/inverter which failed from the shock of chock release. This was supposedly determined from ground tests at the Downey facility. The solution to this problem was the substitution of a new inverter developed for the G-26.

The alternative reason for this problem comes from an NAA engineer at the Cape during this time. According to him the problem was the dead facing of an ambilical. At chock release this ambilical would send a false signal to the computer causing a failure.

An interesting story regarding this problem was some ground tests done on an X-10 at the Cape. Using a tug and tow bar, engineers tried to simulate chock release by jerking the missile forward. With each attempt, the vehicle moved forward out of the hanger until it reached the end of its power cables [with the engines "off" all power came from the hanger]. At this point, the engineers reversed the motion and tried to shock the vehicle while shoving the X-10 back into the hanger. Unfortunately, the tow bar was designed to take tension not compression and snapped during the operation. This failure promptly ended the Cape bounce tests.

X-10 Flight 24

The ninth Cape flight occurred on 27 August 1956. The vehicle was GM 52-1, X-10 number eight. The mission was a straight supersonic flight to the Grand Bahama Island impact area.

Having completed three missions already, number eight had earned the title hanger queen: it always came back. It was because of this that it was selected to complete number nine's dive-in flight. It was this success that also made it difficult to send this vehicle to its destruction.

G-26 number one [GM10989] sits on complex 9 in this rare aerial view. Here we can see the whole complex clearly, particularly the erecting tower. Like the Matador facility, the launcher was aligned to point south not south east. The G-26 was expected to make a course correction right after ramjet ignition. Photo by: U.S. Air Force, Cape Canaveral AFB.

As if to make its last flight more memorable, number eight's takeoff was anything but normal. After leaving the ground and locking the main gear brakes, number eight suddenly settled back to the runway. With its wheels locked the tires quickly overheated and burst. Within seconds number eight was roaring down the runway on its wheel rims, cutting four grooves into the pavement.

If having both main gear tires fail was not bad enough, the main gear also was retracting. As it retracted the main gear doors contacted the pavement carving its own groove. An engineer later noted that you could see the wheel and the door grooves moving towards each other as the retraction sequence progressed. Then, without any obvious reason, number eight lifted upward and cleared the runway.

After this heart stopping lift-off, number eight flew at supersonic speed to its impact point. There it successfully dove into its target island proving that the vehicle's structure could take the strain.

Number eight's epic last flight was the only good thing to happen in the Navaho program during August. Throughout

G-26 number one at night. This is the type of activity that would occur the night before a launch. The photo however is dated 12 September 1956, almost two months before the first flight. At that time the APU was still giving engineers fits. Photo by: U.S. Air Force.

the month problems occurred with booster number three. During pre-chilling for the first static firing, the fiberglass insulation around the LOX tank blistered. The extreme cold of the liquid caused the booster's aluminum skin to shrink away from the insulation. To keep the insulation on for the test, NAA personnel wrapped chair springs around the tank. Much later North American corrected the problem by changing the primer coat used on the aluminum skin.[3]

With springs around the insulation, NAA tried three more times to fire booster number three. One launch attempt was canceled when a helium line ruptured in the kerosene tank. The other test was canceled after the G-26's landing gear extended internally, cracking the missile's keel beam. Only the fourth try on 30 August produced ignition. The test lasted only 2 seconds of its planned 30 before excessive gas generator temperature forced a cutoff.

In September NAA tried three more times to static fire this booster. The first test ended at ignition because range officials could not see if both thrust chambers ignited. The second attempt lasted five of its planned 20 seconds before a missile umbilical cable was accidentally disconnected.

On the third attempt the engine actually ran longer then planned. A malfunction in the missile's APU forced the use of ground power. This switch in power source induced control problems in the booster system. The result was a 30 second engine test that ran for 34 seconds .

This test may have been a successful engine test, but it showed that the APU still was unreliable. This forced another delay in the flight of number one as well as the cancellation of the first Broomstick flight. Until G-26 number one flew, G-26 number four – the first autonavigator equipped G-26 – could not be loaded onto launch complex 9.

X-10 Flight 25

On 21 September 1956 NAA rolled X-10 number 13 out onto the Skid-Strip for the first time. Its mission was to further test the N6 autonavigator unit.

At a distance of 35 nautical miles down range, ground control engaged the N-6A autonavigator. The vehicle then flew under N-6 control for 203 nautical miles towards station 4 [Eleuthera Island]. At this distance the lateral navigation error was only two nautical miles.

Still under autonavigator control, X-10 number 13 then performed a banked turn to the left and headed back to the Cape. Shortly after completing the turn however the missile began losing altitude. Flight telemetry also began showing erroneous Mach and speed readings.

By traveling at only Mach 0.9 and at 39,000 feet, number 13 was collecting ice in its Pitot tube and engines. This not only increased the vehicle's weight, it also effected the engine performance. Only after the vehicle descended to 18,000 feet did the ice begin to melt stopping the vehicle's descent. Vehicle guidance was not effected by this however with the lateral guidance error at this point being only three nautical miles.

By the time X-10 number 13 arrived back at the Cape the lateral error was barely one mile. Ground control then took

over and the vehicle landed using the automatic landing system. The missile touched down 2,500 feet down the Skid Strip and rolled for 5,000 feet until it contacted the barrier. The barrier then functioned properly stopping the X-10 in just 800 feet [minor damage occurred]. Total flight time was one hour 19 minutes, 40 seconds: distance flown 627 miles.

X-10 Flight 26

On 24 October 1956 GM 52-6 again completed a full auto-navigation flight with the N6A guidance system showing its accuracy. No information about lateral error has been published.

G-26 Flight One

Throughout October APU problems prevented the launching of G-26 number one [GM10989]. On 6 November 1956 however the missile was ready for flight. The purpose of the flight was to gather data on booster propulsion and separation characteristics. The flight also was to test flight control, missile flutter and vibration.

Last minute problems extended the countdown from 7.5 hours to 14.4 hours. Then the two booster chambers of

Engine ignition on G-26 number one, 6 November 1956. In seconds the vehicle would leave the pad on its short, but wild, ride. Photo by: U.S. Air Force.

booster 003 ignited. Full thrust was achieved and the missile rose rapidly from the pad.

For ten seconds G-26 number one looked like all the delays and problems had been worth it. Then it began to pitch up and down wildly. The ground controller frantically tried to stabilize the vehicle, but the phugoid[4] oscillation only increased. Structural failure and vehicle explosion then occurred at T plus 26 seconds. The forward and aft sections of the missile, and the engine section of the booster, landed in the ocean 2.5 miles down range.

Post flight analysis showed that the autopilot caused the failure. Technicians at the Autonetics facility had installed the unit's pitch rate gyro backward. This caused it to detect yaw movements, preventing the autopilot from detecting changes in vehicle pitch. All yaw movements however resulted in both a corrective yaw and pitch command.

Regardless of the pitch gyro failure the autopilot did successfully control the vehicle in yaw and roll. Radar plots also showed that the vehicle did maintain the proper heading.

G-26 number one just after liftoff from complex nine. The vehicle is already canted well over in its flight angle. This may well prove the information that the pitch gyro was installed incorrectly and was not controlling pitch at takeoff. Photo by: Dale D. Meyers.

X-10 Flight 27
On 20 November 1956 the last X-10 flight of the Navaho program was completed at the Cape. This time GM 52-6 was to fly out to 50,000 feet and Mach 1.3 and then hit an island. As with the previous flight, the vehicle performed perfectly. This flight marked the end of Phase One of the Navaho test program.

Summary Of Cape X-10 Flights
The X-10 flights at Cape Canaveral set many technological firsts.

(1) The first automatic landing at Cape Canaveral, 3 February 1956.
(2) The first Turbojet powered flight to Mach 2, 29 February 1956.[5]
(3) The first all inertial flight of an unmanned missile, 18 July 1956.
(4) The first all inertial flight of a missile from launch to impact, 20 November 1956.

An extremely sharp picture of number one as it roared skyward. If a person only saw these pictures, the impression would be of a perfect launch. On film however one would see the missile pitching up and down out of control. Photo by: U.S. Air Force.

These are just the accomplishments that would end up in a history book. The X-10 Cape flights however did far more in proving the Navaho design.

(1) Five N-6 autonavigator flights were completed, all gathering test data on the units accuracy and reliability. The results showed that the N-6 had an error of less than a mile after over an hour of operation.
(2) Two X-10's performed the planned dive-in attack method. Both vehicle's structure and control system functioned properly proving the later G-26 and G-38 could perform this maneuver. In a related test flight, an X-10 crashed into the ocean at a speed of Mach 1.25.
(3) The first high angle approach landing was successfully

completed. This was necessary for the successful recovery of the later G-26 missile's. Thirty years later, Space Shuttles would make similar high angle [dead stick] approach landings at the Cape .

(4) Initial testing and calibration of the Cape's first radar tracking system. These tests included tracking a Mach 2 vehicle at altitudes of over 45,000 feet. These tests were essential for the later tracking of the Mach 3, 70,000 feet, G-26s and the various Mach 8, 120,000 feet, ballistic missiles then in construction.

NOTES

(1) The parabrake, plus the differential braking, could stop an X-10 in 3,400 feet. Without it however the vehicle would always over run the runway. All the overruns encountered by X-10 number one at Edwards AFB were due to parabrake failure.

(2) This does not include the Snark that flew to Brazil on 5 December 1956. That missile went off course and never reached Ascension island.

(3) It is unknown whether the fiberglass insulation on this booster was fully repaired before the booster was used to launch the first G-26 missile. Given the time required to strip off the old insulation, remove the original primer, and then recoat, it is likely that the first G-26 flew with chair springs wrapped around its LOX tank.

(4) The word Phugoid is used in engineering to describe a pitching motion.

(5) The first manned fighter to reach Mach 2 in level flight was a prototype Lockheed F-104A Starfighter [YF-104A]. This flight occurred on 27 April 1956, two months after the X-10 flight.

A final color picture of the launch of G-26 number one. This launch serves as the transition point. Navaho Phase One testing is now complete with Phase Two testing underway. It also marks the end of the most successful phase of the Navaho program and the beginning of its tragic end. From this point on there would be few successes culminating in a bitter end. Photo by: William F. Gibson Jr.

Chapter 5
The Final Days

Testing, Phase Two

With the launch of G-26 number one, phase two of the Navaho testing program had begun. North American now loaded the first Broomstick missile onto launch complex 9. The first static firing of booster 009 was set for the first week of December. Following this, the launch of G-26 number four would occur on 17 December 1957. The G-26's tendency for problems however had not ended.

An unidentified G-26 missile/booster combination sits on the launcher at complex 9. Several NAA engineers are standing on the third level of the launcher. Other personnel maybe on the catwalks, several stories higher, checking the instrument compartment. Photo by: Rockwell International.

On 3 December a failure of the missile's N6 autonavigator forced the cancellation of the first static firing. Two days later NAA tried again only to have a lubricant tank malfunction automatically shutdown the engine. A third attempt on 7 December did succeed in reaching booster ignition, but a valve supplying liquid fuel to both the gas generator and the regenerative cooling system failed. A burn through then happened seriously damaging the engine thrust chamber. To make the necessary repairs required removal of the missile from complex 9. As a result, North American had to reschedule the launch to 15 January 1957.

At this point a new problem occurred that threatened to delay the Navaho program even further. Under Air Force regu-

lations, all ground handling equipment used in the program had to undergo periodic static load checks. To do these certification checks required the assistance of the range contractor: Pan American Airlines. North American and Air Force inspectors however were not receiving Pan Am's help as requested. By late 1956 these inspectors were stating they would soon have to "Red Tag" available North American equipment if this situation was not corrected. It has not been reported if this issue was ever solved.

Vehicle number five [8272] in close-up while on the pad at complex nine. Though a little premature to show this picture, this view shows an interesting operation performed on all G-26s. The metal hook on the rudder is used to measure control surface deflection. Prior to a launch the control surfaces were cycled to see if there was any impediment to movement. Note that the canards and the elevons are also being cycled, though no measuring devices are present. Finally, note that the covers are not on the instrument compartment. The structural rings make this area look like it has vents. Photo by: Rockwell International.

On 10 January 1957 North American ended a launch attempt when a small fire started in the left ramjet engine. Later analysis showed that a mismatched connector to the vehicle's APU had started the fire. The damage was minor however and in five days the vehicle was ready for launch. This second attempt reached T minus 3 minutes before ships appeared in the booster impact zone.

The Air Force estimated it would take an hour to clear the ships from the area. Unfortunately, NAA personnel had already disconnected the vehicle's ammonia fill line [used in the internal air-conditioning system]. The G-26's helium supply, used to pressurize the kerosene tank, also was marginal. Given these facts, NAA engineers did not believe they could wait an hour. Thus, the Air Force rescheduled the launch for the next day.

The 16 January launch would actually reach the zero mark. Unfortunately the booster's engines did not ignite. Determination of the failure, repairs and rescheduling took eight days making for a fourth launch attempt on 24 January 1957. This attempt would get down to two minutes thirty seconds when an engineer erroneously reported a loss of power in the APU.

Six days after the engineer's error, on 30 January 1957 G-26 number four [8271] was back on launch complex 9 ready

The erector tower is in the quarter position [whether going down or up is unknown]. Again, this is vehicle number five and booster 007 during the control surface cycling operation. Note the lanyards hanging down from the rear of the flight missile. Photo by: Rockwell International.

for launch. This time however it was not the missile that malfunctioned but the self-destruct package. During a pre-flight test it proved defective, requiring replacement. Since the destruction unit was in the G-26's nose wheel well the missile had to be separated from the booster to gain access. This in turn required removing the missile from the launcher.

While these launch attempts were underway, in January the Air Force placed a hold notice on advertising for the construction of Navaho facilities. This notice ended NAA's efforts to get bids for the construction of a calibration laboratory, an engineering laboratory and launch complexes 27 A and 27B. These new facilities were for use in the G-38 phase of the Navaho program.

On 1 February 1957 North American tried for the sixth time to launch G-26 number four. In this attempt the APU's

igniter [glowplug] failed, leaving the missile with no internal electric power source. Five days later, on 6 February, North American made a seventh attempt. Now a voltage regulator malfunctioned, leaving the missile without a stable electric power source. On 19 February a new electrical problem forced cancellation of the 8th attempt. This time the problem was not with the missile, but with the power plant at Station 10 [San Salvador Island]. This unexpected brown-out killed both the station's radio control system and the radar tracking unit.

As if nothing else could go wrong during a G-26 launch, on 27 February NAA canceled the ninth attempt because of weather. Heavy clouds had moved in during the count down making the optical tracking system useless. The launch was then rescheduled for the tenth time to 1 March 1957. During this attempt the fuel feed valve from the regenerative cooling

A Thor IRBM on a fixed test launcher at the Cape. This is a late model Thor, somewhat different looking than the one that exploded on 25 January 1957. This one has been fueled with liquid oxygen, hence the vapor jet from its side pressure vent. Photo by: U.S. Air Force.

system to the gas generator valve failed to open. Without the gas generator the turbopump would not work and the engine automatically cut-off.

While this was going on, the Air Force disclosed that fiscal year 1958 Navaho funding would be cut. In response to this, in February North American and the Air Force Weapon System Office began studying ways to cut program costs. On 27 February NAA proposed an austere program calling for a 32% cut in funding, the production of only 16 G-26 missile. Also proposed was a delay in the start of G-38 flights from June 1958 to February 1959.

The Competition

To put these problems in proper perspective one should note how other missile programs were doing during these months. On 20 December 1956 Douglas tried to launch its first Thor IRBM. The flight was aborted when the missile's engine did not ignite. On 25 January 1957 Douglas tried again to launch this missile. On engine ignition the missile toppled over and exploded.

Northrop launched eight Snarks between 14 November 1956 and 12 March 1957. Four performed properly and were recovered. Three others completed their flight but crashed on landing. The 8th missile however became the first Snark to reach its maximum range of 5,000 miles. Unfortunately, it did this after it went off course and failed to destruct as commanded. In January of 1983 a Brazilian farmer found it while he was clearing a section of rain forest.

G-26 Flight Two

While NAA personnel fought G-26 number four [8271] , G-26 number two [10990] and booster 006 were ready for launch. Its mission was the same of flight number one, to test out the vehicle's aerodynamics. Originally, this flight also was to test out the planned mobile launcher unit developed by Food Machinery Corporation. The first successful static firing of booster 006 occurred on this launcher in February. A second static firing of 16 second duration occurred on March 12th.

With the booster ready, NAA scheduled the launch for 22 March 1957. NAA also set it up that the launch would occur from complex nine, to minimize the potential for failure. Minor problems did occur however, causing 4.8 hours in holds to the countdown. Finally, after a countdown of 9.8 hours G-26 number 2 roared from complex nine. Immediately, the missile was in trouble.

At lift-off the kerosene start-pod for the booster did not separate. This was caused by a failure of a launch lanyard [cable] to separate from the vehicle on lift-off. As the vehicle accelerated, aerodynamic forces ripped the pod from the booster at 15,000 feet. The damage to the booster was extensive, causing an immediate decay in thrust.

Though now decelerating, the vehicle continued to climb until at 28,300 feet separation occurred. Vehicle speed however was only Mach 1.3, too low to ignite the ramjets. Thus, G-26 number two began an unpowered glide to the sea.

Though ramjet ignition was impossible, the vehicle could still be controlled. The radio command pilot used the missile's airbrakes and control surfaces to regulate speed and glide angle. He even lowered the landing gear before the vehicle hit the ocean approximately 26 miles from the launch site.

The launch of G-26 number two on 22 March 1957. The launch is from complex nine, a fact due to the large fixed launcher shown. Cape Canaveral historical records however state that this missile was launched from complex ten. At that site was the mobile launcher. Photo by: William F. Gibson Jr.

An unidentified G-26 in flight. Like many G-26 flights, this one has yet to release its booster. Photo by: Dale D. Meyers.

A Snark in flight. This is an early test Snark, similar to the one that flew on 16 April 1957. The Snarks always were ahead of the Navaho G-26s in distance flown. So great was the distance flown in April, only the G-38 and the in construction Atlas B could beat the Snark. Photo by: Northrop Aircraft.

The Competition

In March of 1957 an Army Jupiter IRBM failed during launch. On 16 April a Snark completed a flight of 270 minute duration [about 2,400 miles]. Three days later Douglas launched its third Thor IRBM. Though successful, a fault in the Cape's radar tracking system forced its destruction after just 30 seconds of flight.

G-26 Flight Three

With Broomstick missile number four still not ready, in March NAA loaded aerodynamic test vehicle number five [8272] and booster 007 onto complex nine. On March 18th North American tried four times to static fire the booster. In two attempts the booster's ignition link did not burn through and ignite the engines. In the third attempt the gas generator's igniter link failed. Finally, during the fourth attempt, the observer cut off the test due to poor visibility. It would only be on the fifth attempt, 29 March 1957, that the booster burned for 15.6 seconds.

With the booster now tested, North American scheduled a launch for 25 April 1957. Last minute holds stretched the planned five hour countdown to 13.7 hours. Then, when it finally reached zero, came the disaster.

Engine ignition was normal and the vehicle lifted off the pad. Then, just four feet off the pad, the booster engines shut down. The vehicle settled back on to the pad and then fell over backwards. On impact it exploded, destroying itself and damaging the launch pad.

Post flight analysis showed that a control lanyard [cable] was too long. By design, when the launch pad hold downs released, the vehicle had 15 seconds to clear the pad. At the end of this time the control system would send a signal shutting down the engines. To prevent this signal the missile had to have pulled free of the lanyard. On this flight the timer reached zero before the lanyard detached. The rockets shutdown according to design and the rest is history.

Vehicle number five and booster number 007 sit on the launcher at complex nine. This beautiful picture shows clearly the missile, booster, lanyards, and the launcher. The side doors of the launcher are open. Behind these doors were the launcher support equipment. This included a water spray system that cooled the pad's exhaust plume during engine ignition. Photo by: Rockwell International.

The Competition

In early May a Douglas Thor missile failed during launch. Later that month however, on 31 May 1957 an Army Jupiter completed a successful flight of 1,500 miles. This marked the United States first successful launch of an IRBM.

Northrop launched three Snarks from 3 May to 20 June 1957. The first broke up 25 miles down range and the second crashed during landing. The last missile[the 1st production prototype] suffered a polarity reversal in a gyro causing it to crash.

On 11 June 1957, Convair launched the first Atlas A ICBM. A booster engine failure forced range safety official to issue the destruction order after just one minute of flight. It had only reached an altitude of 10,500 feet.

A long distance picture of an unidentified G-26 launch. This was as far as number five got before the engines cut out. Moments later the vehicle toppled over and exploded. Photo by: U.S. Air Force.

A Jupiter IRBM sits on its mobile launch pad at the Cape. The Jupiter was the only strategic U.S. ballistic missile system to be mobile. Its simple yet rugged design made it a far better weapon then the competing Thor IRBM. Photo by: U.S. Air Force.

By April the G-26 program had attempted 15 launches with only two actually leaving the base area. These failures had prompted Northrop personnel to name the missile "Never-Go-Navaho." This title was not amusing to the North American engineers, or to the Air Force. To get the program back on track, in April NAA and the directorate of test Engineering [AFMTC] began a comprehensive reliability study of the G-26 system. This study recommended several improvements which NAA incorporated into all remaining missiles and the ground equipment.

With the study in hand, in May North American proposed a new Navaho construction plan. In this new plan North American would build launch complexes 27A and 27B and a small assembly building [building Q] for the G-38. AFMTC countered however with a proposal for the modification of complexes 9 and 10 instead. Surprisingly, AFMTC staff viewed this plan less favorably than the NAA plan. One concern was the delays it would cause in the start of the G-38 test program. Another concern was the lack of back-up facilities in case of a launch failure like that of G-26 number five.

At the request of the AFMTC, on 29 May 1957 Colonel F A Holm, Chief of the Navaho Weapons System Project Office, presented several alternative plans to AFMTC. One plan proposed modifying complex 10 for launching the G-38 while leaving complex 9 for the completion of the G-26 program. These and other plans were then submitted to Headquarters, U.S. Air Force Air Research and Development Command for final decision.

G-26 Flight Four

It took until mid-June to repair complex 9 and load G-26 missile number three [8270] and booster number 008. Because booster number 008 had already been fired [8 April 1957 on the mobile launcher], no additional test was needed. This allowed NAA to accelerate the launch schedule and set the launch for 21 June.

The 21 June launch would be aborted before booster ignition. So would a second launch attempt on 25 June. During the third attempt on 26 June 1957 however, everything worked perfectly. Missile number three [8270] roared from the launcher to test vehicle aerodynamics during boost, separa-

Here we see vehicle number five again with the erector tower around it. The tower was called the Taj Mahal by the engineers. It allowed access to virtually any part of the missile when erect. Photo by: Rockwell International.

tion and cruise flight. It also was instrumented to gather data on ramjet operation and the missile's fuel control system.

After a normal takeoff, the missile and booster functioned properly for about 42 seconds, reaching 23,500 feet and Mach 1.63. Then a fire occurred in the rocket engine compartment causing a premature thrust decay. Later analysis of telemetry data showed that one of the valves going from the regenerative cooling system to the gas generator had closed. The failure of a gas generator would in turn cause a turbopump to fail, causing the loss of one engine.

Now with booster power deteriorating, the vehicle coasted upward to an altitude of 40,000 feet. There booster separation occurred successfully, releasing the missile for cruise flight. Since the G-26 never reached start speed for the Wright ramjets however, all the ground controller could do was select landing mode and gather data on the G-26's glide characteristics. The vehicle fell into the ocean 47 nautical miles from the launch point.

Seventeen days after this G-26 flight, on 13 July 1957 the Air Force canceled the Navaho program. The limited success of the first Atlas flight, the success of the Jupiter IRBM and the continued problems with the G-26 forced this decision. From that day forward the Air Force emphasized the development of ballistic missile systems.

The cancellation of the program was a major blow to North American Aviation. In February of 1957 NAA had released

G-26 number three [8270] and booster 008 during its launch. The last of the original Navaho launches it looks great at this point. 42 seconds later at 23,500 feet a fire erupted internally. Having only reached Mach 1.6, slower then an X-10, its primary accomplishment was the testing of the landing system. The picture though is extremely clear showing quite a bit of vehicle detail. Photo by: Rockwell International.

the G-38 design for production. Key sub-assemblies were in testing at the Missile Division in Downey. NAA also was set to begin mass production of the Rocketdyne booster engines, and the Autonetics Autopilot and N6B Autonavigator. Other companies primed for production were Wright Aeronautical [ramjets], Thompson Products [APU] and Food Machinery Corp. [mobile launcher].

Before the first week was out, 4,705 people were laid off from North American's Downey, Anaheim, and Canoga Park facilities. Within a month the Missile Division lost 7,000 people while Autonetics lost up to 3,000 people. Total personnel reduction was expected to reach 15,600 at four NAA facilities.

Though the Air Force had canceled the program, permission was given to launch five of the remaining G-26 missiles. The mission was to gather additional data on the high temperature environment encountered at Mach 2.75. The tests

Unfinished G-26 missiles and boosters at the Downey Division of North American Aviation. At least seven missiles and 12 booster frames are in this picture. A few of these would be finished and sent to the Cape for Fly-Five and the RISE programs. Also in the left side of the picture are the pieces of the G-38 booster. Note the extra large tube frame and the polished pyramid pieces The polished pieces are the bulkheads for the G-38 fuel tanks. Photo by: North American Chronology.

also were to gather data on stability and control of a supersonic canard vehicle, and evaluation of the N6 inertial guidance system. Expenditures for these tests were not to exceed 4.9 million dollars. These flights are know as the Fly-Five series.

Flight 5
Before the cancellation, in early June NAA personnel loaded the first Broomstick missile onto the mobile launcher. Static testing of booster 009 then began on 13 June with two test firings. During the initial test, automatic shutdown occurred when a sensor showed high gas generator temperature. Post test analysis showed that the reading was due to a broken lead to a thermocouple. NAA personnel replaced the thermocouple, following which the booster was fired for 15 seconds.

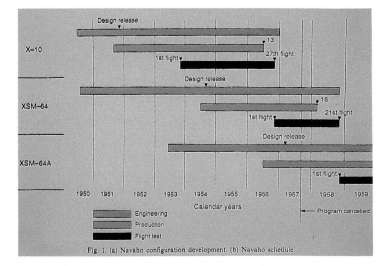

Fig. 1. (a) Navaho configuration development. (b) Navaho schedule.

Left: A time line for Weapon System 104A. Here shows the start of the X-10, G-26 and G-38 programs. These time lines show the start/finish of engineering, construction, and testing for all three missiles. The only activity not listed is the short X-10 Drone program. Photo by: Author.

After two additional firings to check the booster ignition sequencer, the missile was prepared for launch. Minor problems forced NAA to cancel two launches in July, pushing the next attempt back to August. During this scheduled launch minor problems extended the countdown from 9.5 hours to

Several pictures of the mobile launcher at complex ten. The missile was G-26 number four on booster 009. The date of these pictures is 6 May 1957 unless otherwise noted. Clockwise from left: (A) A view of an erect G-26 from the mobile erecting arm that locked around the G-26 booster body.
(B) A top view of the G-26 on the launcher. Though hidden behind the missile, the erecting arm is still connected to the missile. Note the fuel and electrical lines which wrap around the port engine intake and then run up the vehicle's nose.
(C) The G-26 from the side, erector arm down and ambilicals disconnected. The missile is essentially ready for launch. The launcher had twin, opposing, exhaust vents instead of the one vent used on the fixed launcher.
(D) The G-26 in the transport position. This picture was taken on 3 May 1957. Unlike the fixed launcher access to vehicle systems was through portable stairs and ladders. This particular picture also shows the use of a crane to lower the G-26 missile onto the booster. Photo by: National Archives.

15.3. None of the problems forced cancellation however and on 12 August 1957 G-26 number four [53-8271] roared from the mobile launcher. Its target was the island of St Lucia in the Windward chain.

After a normal lift-off, the autonavigator placed the missile on the proper flight path for St Lucia. At booster cut-off however the guidance system malfunctioned and would not release the vehicle until the combination reached an altitude of 81,000 feet. This high boost trajectory induced large amplitude phugoid [Pitch] oscillations into the vehicle's flight path. The autopilot quickly damped out these oscillations, following which the Wright ramjets were ignited for the first time.

Under ramjet power the vehicle maintained a speed of Mach 2.93 for over 150 miles. Then the missile began drifting off course. Ground control took over to bring the vehicle back on line but the maneuver caused the vehicle's body to blank

A Soviet SS-9 ICBM is lowered into its silo during the 1960s. Though not the missile flown in 1957 it shows the same Soviet missile philosophy: lots of motors. Unable to develop the Navaho style high thrust motors, they compensated with many small engines. The 1957 booster had twenty thrust chambers, each producing only 50,000 lbs of thrust. A Navaho chamber produced twice that amount. Photo by: U.S. Dept of Defense.

An unidentified G-26 during launch. Photo by: William F. Gibson Jr.

out the left ramjet inlet. Unable to take in enough air to maintain combustion, the ramjet failed just 7.5 minutes into the flight.

Without the left engine the G-26 began decelerating rapidly. Within a minute the right engine failed leaving the missile without thrust. At this point Range Safety officials ordered the missile placed into a terminal dive for destruction. Thus, at T plus 9 minutes 26 seconds number four crashed into deep water just off Great Abaco Island in the Bahamas. It had only completed 230 of its planned 1,550 mile flight.

On 20 August 1957 the Soviet Union announced that they had successfully launched and controlled an ICBM. Because this launch was completely over Soviet territory there was no evidence it even occurred. Thus, the government dismissed it as propaganda.

G-26 Flight 6

Just days before the cancellation, North American delivered G-26 number six [54-3095] to the Cape. On 19 July its booster, number 10, was static fired on launch complex 9. The two

A late model Atlas during launch at the Cape. The first successful Atlas A flight was on 17 December 1957 [it went 800 miles]. The first successful 6,325 mile flight occurred a year later on 28 November 1958. The missile then went operational in September of 1959, one year earlier then Navaho was planned to. Photo by: U.S. Air Force.

vehicles were then mated and a launch set for 18 September 1957. Like the previous missile, it was to fly to St Lucia and then dive into the ocean.

The launch of G-26 number six was one of the best yet in the Navaho series. Separation was at 77,000 feet as planned with the ramjets successfully igniting immediately after. Maximum speed reached was Mach 3.5 with a sustained speed of Mach 3.0. Then, after fifteen minutes of flight and a distance of 450 miles, a nine degree turn to the right occurred. Ground control took over, but then a ramjet blow-out occurred.

With the missile now unpowered and dropping the ground controller at Station 5 [San Salvador Island] had no choice but to initiate a dive-in. After 18 minutes 57 seconds, number six hit the ocean 500 miles down range SE of the Acklins.

On 25 September 1957 the second flight rated Atlas A missile was launched. It held together for 3 minutes before Range Safety officials triggered the destruction unit. Four days later the Soviet Union launched Sputnik.

Following Sputnik, no one in the United States government or the Air Force would even talk about the Navaho or cruise missiles in general. Fly Five would continue, but the emphasis now was on getting an ICBM into service. So strong was this attitude that when the first Snark reached Ascension Island on 31 October it was essentially ignored.[1]

G-26 number five without the erecting tower. Note the twin lanyards going from the ramjet exhaust down to the launcher. Photo by: Rockwell International.

An N-69 Snark during launch. This is the same type as the one that reached Ascension island. Photo by: Northrop.

An unidentified G-26 in-flight. This black and white photo was taken from a color transparency. The transparency however has yellowed, losing much of its color. Photo by: William F. Gibson Jr.

Flight 7

With complex 9 clear, in late September NAA delivered missile number seven [54-3096] and booster 011. Static testing of the booster began on 2 October with a burn of 5.25 seconds. This test ended prematurely when an observer noted abnormally low temperature readings in the gas generator. No damage occurred however and the flight was scheduled for 13 November 1957.

Like the previous flights it was to test boost and separation, ramjet ignition, inertial guidance & flight control, and overall aerodynamic performance. In addition, the missile was to gather vibration and temperature data for the ramjet engine and guidance system compartments.

The launch of number seven was one of the least eventful of the Navaho program. In all, technical holds only amounted to 2.5 hours of the 12 hour countdown. The launch was normal with booster separation occurring at 67,000 feet and at a speed of Mach 3.24.

At this point an erratic voltage regulator caused the loss of all missile telemetry. This prevented the ground control from knowing whether the ramjets ignited or not [optical tracking cameras would later show they did]. Thus, at T plus 75 seconds, ground control issued the destruction order ending the flight.

Flight 8

In September of 1957 North American Aviation delivered ve-

A nice color picture of an unidentified G-26. No booster numbers, and no way to see the fin numbers. Finally, all G-26s had the same bright insignia orange paint job, unlike the X-10s which varied from vehicle to vehicle. This missile seems to be ready for flight with the instrument compartment closed. Photo by: Rockwell International.

A stern view of a G-26 in flight. Photo by: William F. Gibson Jr.

(1) It was the longest [42 minutes 28 seconds] inertially guided flight.
(2) It was the longest atmospheric flight at speeds over Mach 2.5. Unofficially, the G-26 won the Bleriot endurance trophy for flying at over 2000 kilometers per hour for more then 30 minutes.[2]

hicle number nine [54-3098] and booster 013. A successful static firing of the booster occurred in November, following which the fourth flight of Fly-Five was set for 10 January 1958.

The goals of this flight was the same as Flight 7. A major difference however was that the missile would be at a higher gross weight at boost and initial cruise. This would show the G-26's growth potential: ability to carry greater scientific or military payloads. The target area was Puerto Rico.

After launch [delayed 2.5 hours], separation occurred at 73,000 feet and Mach 3.15. Ramjet ignition then followed and the vehicle began its cruise flight towards a point in the Atlantic. Unlike previous flights, the missile would make it to this point.

Number nine would function properly for forty minutes, more than twice as long as any other G-26. At a sustained speed of Mach 2.8 the vehicle would cover a distance of 1,075 miles. The N6 guidance unit then executed a right turn to bring the missile back to the Cape. Then the problem happened.

Real time radar data showed that the missile was not turning fast enough. Ground control took over and increased the rate of turn. As in previous flights the turn blanked out the right engine causing failure. The radio command system then executed a manual dive ending the flight.

Though this G-26 flight was classed only a marginal success, it set many records.

An unidentified G-26 on the launcher at complex nine. Note the huge bottle rack of helium. Photo by: Dale D. Meyers.

(3) The first G-26 to fly 1,000 miles.
(4) The telemetry system function properly sending data on external and internal temperatures. Also data on guidance system functions, booster engine performance and vibration.

Flight 9

The last of the Fly-Five boosters, number 12, arrived at the Cape in December of 1957. The first successful static firing of the booster occurred in mid-January of 1958. The missile, vehicle number 8 [54-3097], arrived that same month. The two units were mated on the launcher and a launch was set for 25 February.

The objectives of this flight were the same as for the previous G-26 flight but without the autonavigator. Though the missile was successfully launched, at T plus 20 seconds the booster shutdown. Separation did not occur and the G-26 was destroyed by radio command.

Project RISE [Research Into Supersonic Environment].

Several months after the end of the Fly-Five series the Air Force began a new program to expend the seven remaining G-26 missiles. Called project RISE it was to extend our knowl-

G-26 number 14 and booster number four sit on the pad at complex nine for the second rise launch. The missile has not even been painted in the standard Navaho orange. It does however have its Navaho logo just behind the canard. If you wish to see it better see the picture of number 14 in Chapter three. Photo by: U.S. Air Force, Cape Canaveral.

edge of supersonic flight environment. The data gathered would be used in the design of the Mach 3 XB-70 bomber and the F-108 Mach 3 interceptor.

Flight 10

On 11 September 1958 the first RISE G-26 was launched from the Cape. The missile was G-26 number 15 [55-4223] and the booster was number 014.

After a successful launch, separation occurred as planned. A fuel system problem then occurred however preventing ramjet ignition. Impact was some 82 miles down range.

Flight 11

The second flight of the RISE program occurred on 18 November 1958. The missile was G-26 number 14 [55-4222] and the booster was number 4. The launch was successful but the vehicle broke up at 77,000 feet.

The failure of the second G-26 canceled all future RISE launches of this missile. Thus, this was the last G-26 ever launched.

The engine exhaust is just exiting the launcher on this unidentified G-26 launch. Photo by: National Archives.

X-10 Drone

In addition to the RISE program, in 1958 the Air Force began the X-10 Drone program. The plan was to use the three remaining missiles as targets for the Bomarc and Nike surface-to-air missiles. The view was that this missile, and the canceled Regulus II, represented the most difficult aerial target possible. To put it simply, the X-10 was the acid test for these interceptor missiles.

A Bomarc missile rises from its Cape launcher. After the RISE program the three remaining Cape X-10s were expended as targets for this missile. Only one of the three flights resulted in an intercept, the first. The other two failed because of problems with both missiles. Photo by: U.S. Air Force.

Drone Flight 1

The first Drone flight occurred on 24 September 1958. The X-10 used in this test was number 12 [GM52-5] which had been used in the autonavigator tests.

After a successful takeoff, number 12 flew out an undisclosed distance and then headed back towards the Cape at high speed. At this point an unarmed Bomarc A was launched on an intercept vector. According to radar plots, the test missile came close enough to the X-10 to destroy the drone. The X-10 was then brought back to the skid-strip.

On landing the parabrake failed and the barrier did not activate. X-10 number 12 then ran off the runway, broke its nose wheel and exploded in flames. The drone's film cam-

X-10 number 12 [GM 52-5], a burned out hulk at the end of the skid strip. This is what happened when the parabrake and the barrier failed. Note that the fire centered around the nose wheel well and engine inlets. Also note the bent back nose wheel under the missile. Photo by: William F. Gibson Jr.

era, used to record the approach of the Bomarc, was destroyed in the fire.

Drone Flight 2

The second drone flight was on 13 November 1958. The X-10 used in this test was number seven [GM-19313]. This was the first flight of this X-10 vehicle.

Takeoff and target run were successful, though unnecessary. The Air Force could not launch the Bomarc A due to problems with the missile. X-10 number seven was then returned to the Cape for a perfect approach and landing. Following touch down however the drag chute failed and the barrier did not activate. Moments later the vehicle was a burning mass at the end of the runway.

Drone Flight 3

The third drone flight was on 26 January 1959[3]. The vehicle involved was X-10 number 10 [GM 52-3]. This was the first flight of this X-10 vehicle.

Takeoff was normal and number 10 headed out to make its target run. The vehicle then suffered a catastrophic failure in its one electrical generator [the second generator had been removed due to a lack of spare parts]. Without electrical power there was no guidance system. The auto-destruct package then fired 30 seconds after the power loss causing the vehicle to crash 57 miles down range. This was the last flight of the X-10 drone program.

At the end of Project RISE and the X-10 Drone program five G-26 and one X-10 still existed. Only one of these G-26s had been delivered to the Cape before RISE was canceled. It was turned over to the base, becoming one of the first exhibits in the Cape Canaveral missile park. As of 1995 it is still reported to be on display.

A similar fate occurred for the last X-10, vehicle number one [19307]. In the fall of 1957 it was donated to the U.S. Air

Force Museum at Wright-Patterson AFB. Today, it sits proudly in the far corner of the museum annex.

As for the four remaining G-26s and boosters, North American put them in storage at the Downey facility. Also stored were the jigs and fixtures for making the missiles as required by U.S. law.[4] Over the next four years NAA produced several different proposals for using the remaining boosters. These proposals ranged from a Thor Able style satellite launch vehicle to a four unit cluster to place North American's X-15 rocket plane into orbit. It also is possible that the remaining G-26 missiles were proposed as high speed target or reconnaissance drones.

On 21 January 1961 the final Navaho document was signed. Soon after this all four remaining G-26 missiles and their boosters were sold as contaminated scrap.

X-10 number one on display at Wright Patterson AFB in the Annex. The Annex is only open on weekdays and you must get a pass from the main museum to get past the Air Force base guard gate. Photo by: Author.

A final look at the G-26s placed in storage after the Navaho was cancelled. One was expended in project RISE. Another became the display missile at Cape Canaveral. The remaining four had the roof of this storage building collapse on them during a heavy California rain in 1958. After that they were stored out side until 1961 when they were all sold as contaminated scrap. Photo by: North American Chronology

NOTES

(1) This Snark flight was the first to use the planned stellar inertial guidance system. Even with the star tracker updates however its lateral error was six nautical miles. This incident shows clearly the problem of gyroscopic precession in long duration flights [eight hours].

(2) In the mid-60s a B-58 Hustler bomber officially won this trophy by completing a 30 minute flight at about 1,250MPH or Mach 2.5. The author uses the term "officially" since the Lockheed A-12 blackbird had been in flight testing since 1962 and easily could have won the trophy. Since its existence was "Secret" however it too could not claim the award.

(3) After the loss of four X-10s for failing to engage the original barrier, North American designed a second barrier. It was first erected for use in this X-10 flight, but its effectiveness was never tested.

(4) Generally, federal law requires government contractors to maintain the jigs and tools for making a weapon system for five years after program termination. This allows for reactivation of a program if the nation's military situation quickly changes. One such event was the cancellation and then ractivation of the Rockwell B-1 bomber program.

The last G-26, number unknown, stands erect at the Cape Canaveral missile park. It is reported that the missile will soon be brought down for refurbishment. Though made mostly of stainless steel, salt air from the ocean has caused significant corrosion. Photo by: Author.

Chapter 6

The Legacy

Testing of Navaho vehicles may have ended, but Navaho technology would live on. The engineering technology developed in this program had both military and civilian uses. Aerodynamic data gathered in the flight tests was used to design new high speed aircraft. Materials developed for the G-38 also found uses in new aircraft designs [subsonic and supersonic]. Even the electronics had multiple uses.

The following are some of the uses Navaho technology has been put to in the last forty years.

Hound Dog

The Hound Dog Air-Launched Cruise Missile was under development before the Air Force canceled the Navaho program. North American developed it to meet an Air Force General Operational Requirement [GOR 148] issued on 15 March 1956. The plan was to give the then four year old B-52 a stand-off attack capability.

On 8 July 1957 North American proposed a design for this missile. The major selling point of the design was the use of as much "off-the-shelf" technology as possible. This was to reduce development costs as well as lower the risk of having a major program delay.

A Hound Dog cruise missile flies over the White Sands Missile Range in New Mexico. The Hound Dog is by all accounts the legitimate child of the Navaho. Its airframe, planform, guidance and autopilot came from the Navaho test vehicles. It would serve as a strategic missile longer than the Atlas. Photo by: U.S. Air Force.

The Hound Dog was a miniature version of the G-38 missile. The wing planform came from the wing of the X-10 test vehicle. The body shape was similar to that of the proposed G-38 missile including the canard and the single tail. Guidance and control were by a modified N6 autonavigator and

PIX10 autopilot. This N6 unit used stellar updates from a Kollsman startracker built into the B-52 wing pylon.

The Air Force issued North American the development contract on 21 August 1957. Winning this contract saved many North American jobs and kept the Missile Division in business. Production of test vehicles began immediately and by November 1958 drop tests were underway. The first powered flight occurred on 23 April 1959. The first N6 guided flight followed six months later.

The Hound Dog entered service on 21 December 1959. Almost immediately it enhanced the effectiveness of the B-52. Its small size and high Mach speed made it almost unstoppable. Its guidance system allowed for turns, dog legs and other evasive maneuvers to confuse radar. Finally, the N6 autonavigator was more reliable and accurate than the bomber's radar navigation system.

For over a decade the Hound Dog was the primary weapon of the B-52. Then in the early 1970s the Air Force deployed the SRAM missile. With this missile came a complete upgrade to the bomber's avionics. By 1975 the Hound Dog was completely outdated and almost incompatible with the B-52 new avionic systems. The missile was then retired

The USS Nautilus underway. The Nautilus and all later U.S. nuclear submarines benefited from Navaho guidance technology. Because of the NAVAN concept, these submarines could accurately determine there geographic position without having to surface. Photo by: United States Naval Institute.

from active duty in 1976. The Air Force demilitarized the last missile on 15 June 1978.

The Hound Dog was a direct child of the Navaho program. It lasted in service for 17 years, twice as lons as the Atlas. Its longevity showed how advanced Navaho technology was.

Inertial Guidance
Nautilus

Soon after the cancellation, the Navy selected the N6 autonavigator for use on the nation's first nuclear powered submarine: the USS Nautilus. The Navy planned to sail this submarine from the Pacific to the Atlantic Ocean via the North

The Nautilus control room during the North Pole journey. With N-6 type guidance units and nuclear reactors U.S. submarines could stay underwater indefinitely. The only limitation is the crews ability to stand long duration confinement. Photo by: United States Naval Institute.

Pole. Such a journey required an Inertial Navigation Unit because standard magnetic compasses become erratic near the magnetic pole of the earth.

The environment of the Nautilus's journey also required a guidance unit that did not use star tracking [totally inertial]. The reason for this was simple: if you have three feet of ice over your head how can you see the stars. This factor made the inertial plus star tracking unit developed by Northrop and other companies inoperable.

Installation of the N6 began in mid-April of 1958. After some initial tests, the submarine began preparations for the polar journey. Then, in late September the Nautilus entered the Arctic Ocean through the Bearing Strait.

As a hedge against malfunctions, the Autonetic's division sent engineers Tom Curtis and George Briston with the Nautilus crew. Their services were not necessary however and at 11:15 PM ET on 3 August 1958 the Nautilus reached the North Pole. A few days later the Nautilus surfaced in the Atlantic Ocean becoming the first ship to traverse the Arctic Ocean.

Polaris

The success of the Nautilus journey, duplicated by the Skate and Seawolf submarines, proved the reliability of the N6 sys-

A Polaris A3 breaks the surface at the start of its 2,500 mile flight [March 1965]. To be accurate, these missiles require the precise location of its launch point. Today, as it was thirty years ago, a NAVAN style INU delivers that location information. Photo by: U.S. Navy.

Left: A Nautilus Ship's Position report made at the moment the submarine crossed the geographic North Pole [3 August 1958]. Note the references to the N-6A unit. Also note the comment "Longitude, Indefinite". Photo by: United States Naval Institute.

The Fleet Ballistic Missile submarine USS James Monroe (SSBN-622) at sea on 6 December 1976. This type of Poseidon submarine carried two N-7 SINS units with Electrostatically Supported Gyro Monitor [ESGM]. Though improved in performance over the original N-6, these units still have a NAVAN baseline. Photo by: U.S. Navy.

tem. Thus, in 1958 the Navy selected an improved unit for use in its Polaris ballistic missile submarines.

Ballistic missile submarines generally launch their missiles from underwater. To make the missiles accurate however, the crew must know the ship's exact location in relation to the target. Before the development of the N6, this could only be done by surfacing and taking a stellar fix. And to do that would give away the ship's location to enemy anti-submarine warships.

Since size and weight were no longer an issue, Autonetics began development of an enhanced N6 unit. Called the N7 autonavigator by Autonetics, the Navy designated the unit the Mk2 SINS [Submarine Inertial Navigation System]. The six George Washington class of Fleet Ballistic Missile submarines, our first Polaris submarines, each carried three of these units.

A Redstone missile can just be seen over its engine exhaust a split second before liftoff. The rocket engine for the Redstone was a major legacy of the Navaho. Powered by this engine, this missile would be the first U.S. space launch vehicle. Photo by: U.S. Army, Redstone Arsenal.

Today Mk2 Mod 7 SINS units are in service on Navy Ohio class [Trident] ballistic missile submarines. Though highly advanced versions of the original Mk2 units, the baseline NAVAN design is the same. Thus, Navaho program technology will serve our nation's defense forces well into the next century.

A-5 Vigilante

Though not as important as the SINS system, the Navaho guidance technology was also used in the North American Aviation A-5 Vigilante. One of the selling points of this Navy strategic bomber was its advanced avionics which included one of the first Head-Up-Displays. The Radar Equipped Inertial Navigation System or REINS was another innovative system designed off N-6 technology.

The A-5 Vigilante served as a Navy strike bomber from 1961 to 1963. After that a reconnaissance version called the RA-5C served into the 1980s.

An A-5 Vigilante during landing approach somewhere in the Atlantic [14 May 1975]. Built by the Columbus Division of North American Aviation, this aircraft used Navaho developed electronics and guidance technology. It would serve the Navy for two decades: first as a bomber, then as a long range reconnaissance aircraft. In this last role, precise guidance was a must to make the photography useful. Photo by: Rockwell International.

The Jupiter C with the Explorer One satellite on top sits fueled for launch [31 January 1958]. With the launching of this satellite, this Redstone variant opened space to the United States and our allies. From that day forward America's space program, at least most of it, has flown on Rocketdyne engines. Photo by: U.S. Army, White Sands.

Rocket Propulsion
Redstone

As noted earlier, one early spin-off of the Navaho program was the engine for the Redstone missile. This engine's reliability would make the Redstone one of the most famous missiles in American rocketry.

From its first flight on 20 August 1953 until its deployment on 14 March 1956, the Redstone set the benchmark for U.S. ballistic missiles. This includes the 1956 flight of a Jupiter A test missile that reached a distance of 3,000 miles.

An early Jupiter IRBM roars skyward. The Jupiter's Rocketdyne engine was developed directly from the later Navaho engines. Years later it would be enhanced into the H1 engine that powered the early Saturn 1B space ship that tested the Apollo capsule. Photo by: U.S. Army.

As a result of its high reliability, in 1957 the U.S. Atomic Energy Commission selected the Redstone to carry a nuclear warhead into the stratosphere. The first such test was on 31 July 1958 from Johnston Island in the Pacific. The Redstone successfully carried its warhead to an altitude of 250,000 feet where it was detonated. Coded name shot Teak, the blast was seen 700 miles away in Honolulu and blacked-out Australian radar for nine hours. A second shot, coded named Orange occurred on 11 August 1958. It was less disruptive due to a lower detonation altitude.

In addition to the nuclear tests, in 1957 the NACA selected the Redstone as the secondary launcher for the first U.S. satellite. After the pad explosion of the first Vanguard missile, on 31 January 1958 a modified Redstone [Jupiter C] launched Explorer one. The missile would then be used to launch Explorer III and IV.

After the explorer launches, the NACA [Later NASA] selected the Redstone to test simulated Mercury capsules. After several tests, in 1961 Redstones carried into space Astronauts Alan Shepard and Gus Grissom in the two Mercury

An Atlas expendable launch vehicle [ELV] roars skyward from the Cape. Only because the Navaho program produced high thrust engines was this missile possible. Today it is still being used to launch military and civilian satellites. Photo by: Rocketdyne.

An even more powerful Atlas Centaur roars from a Cape launch complex. The Atlas was the workhorse of the early U.S. space program, carrying both satellites and the Mercury astronauts. Today, it is a middle to heavy range booster behind the Titan IV and the Rocketdyne-engined Space Shuttle. Photo by: Rocketdyne.

Sub-orbital missions. Two years later the United States Army retired it from service.

Jupiter

The rocket engine used by the Jupiter IRBM also was a Navaho spin-off. It would serve with the United States Air Force from 11 July 1960 to mid-1964. More importantly the Jupiter's engine links the Navaho program with the Apollo program.

In addition to its use as an IRBM, NACA developed a satellite launch vehicle from the Jupiter. Called the Juno, in

1958 it successfully launched the deep space probe Pioneer III. In 1959 it also placed Pioneer IV in orbit around the sun, and Pioneer VII into earth orbit.

In 1958 NACA asked Rocketdyne to develop an advanced version of the Jupiter engine. The plan was to develop a high thrust rocket to place a three man crew into earth orbit. The engine that came from this was the H1 that served as the first stage engine for the Saturn S1B launch vehicle.

That same year Rocketdyne also began development of the largest liquid oxygen and kerosene engine ever flown. Called the F1, five of these engines lifted the enormous Saturn V moon rocket off the pad. Thus, the F1 engine is a direct descendent of the rocket engine used in the G-26 test missile.

Atlas

Though its development caused Navaho's cancellation, the Atlas owned much to this program. Without Navaho, its MA-2 propulsion system could not have been developed until 1959.

The Atlas began service with the Air Force in 1959. The Air Force deployed three models, the last two incorporating inertial guidance systems. Then in 1965 the Air Force retired them in favor of the Minuteman missile.

The Atlas also has civilian uses. On 18 December 1958 an Atlas carrying a radio unit transmitted President Eisenhower's taped Christmas message to the world. On 20 February 1962 an upgraded Atlas using MA-5 engines [enhanced MA-2s] carried John Glenn into earth orbit. Many other commercial and military payloads have since been carried into orbit.

Today, Atlas 2AS ELVs [Expendable Launch Vehicles] are in service launching satellites. This booster is the third largest satellite launch vehicle in U.S. service, and one of the most reliable.

Thor

The Thor IRBM's engine was a modified version of the Atlas ICBM's booster engine. Thus, it too was a spin-off of Navaho research.

The Thor had the longest nuclear history of any Navaho spin-off. From 1959 to 1964 the United States Air Force operated the Thor as a strategic nuclear weapon. In 1962 the AEC used the Thor to carry a Hydrogen bomb to an altitude of 280 miles. Its detonation turned night into day for six minutes over Hawaii. Finally, from 1962 to 1967, it served as a nuclear tipped anti-satellite weapon. Deployed on launchers at Vandenberg AFB and Kawajalein Atoll, it defended the nation against surveillance satellites.

In addition to its military uses, the Thor also became a satellite launch vehicle. Tailored to earth orbital missions, the Thor Able would set the standard for reliability. In the late 1970s the engine was enhanced and redesignated the RS-27. The vehicle as well, constantly being improved was renamed the Delta. Today, Delta II rockets regularly carry commercial satellites into earth orbit.

A Thor IRBM roars from its launch site at Cape Canaveral. The Thor had a long career as a military rocket and an even longer one as a satellite launch vehicle. Its engine was an Atlas booster engine which in turn was developed from the Navaho engine. Photo by: McDonnell-Douglas.

At the time of this writing McDonnell-Douglas is planning an upgraded Delta designated Delta III. This new vehicle is to have an enlarged fuselage allowing for greater fuel capacity. Expected maximum payload to earth orbit is 8,000 pounds or four tons. Thus, the Navaho legacy should continue to live on in our space program well into the 21st century.

Gimballed Rocket Engines

The G-38 booster engine would also be the first large rocket unit to have gimballed engines. Prior to this booster the method used to vector thrust was jet vanes placed in the engine's exhaust stream. These vanes were inefficient, and eroded during engine burn reducing their effectiveness during flight.

The gimballed system pioneered with the G-38 motor was more effective and maintained its effectiveness throughout engine burn. This maintaining of effectiveness through flight would make it the primary thrust vectoring system of later

An Atlas engine cluster being static fired at Santa Susanna. Originally built for the Navaho program, the Santa Susanna facility continues to develop and test rocket engines. Thus, another Navaho legacy is the infrastructure needed to continue the advancement of aerospace technology. Photo by: Rocketdyne.

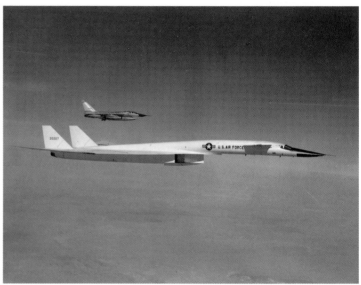

An XB-70 Valkyrie bomber in flight, 3 November 1965. This bomber prototype is still the largest supersonic aircraft to ever fly. Much of its design can be traced to the Navaho test vehicles of the previous decade. Photo by: U.S. Air Force.

Left: Today, the Thor lives on in the form of the Delta II. The Delta launch vehicle is the primary mid-range booster behind the Atlas. Its engine is an uprated version of the Thor engine called a RS-27. A new larger version called the Delta III is in development. Whether it will use the RS-27 is still being considered but this Navaho based engine still has a few years left in the U.S. Space Program. Photo by: McDonnell-Douglas.

manned space vehicles. From the Saturn V moon rocket to the three engine cluster of the Space shuttle, gimballed engines are a major legacy of the Navaho missile program.

High Speed Aerodynamics

Data gathered by the X-10 and G-26 vehicles improved our understanding of high speed flight environment. High speed parasite drag, wave drag, aero elasticity and aerothermal heating are specific areas where the Navaho program increased our technical knowledge. This data would then be used to design more efficient aircraft, allowing faster speeds or greater distances. Today even manned fighters use the X-10's planform.

X-15

One program that benefited from the Navaho was the North American X-15 program. In 1954 the NACA and the Air Force called for proposals for a Mach 3+, 60,000 feet+ test aircraft. Bell aircraft and Douglas submitted designs for this vehicle. Both companies had extensive experience in making high speed rocket planes with their X-1, and D-558 aircraft.

Though not a primary competitor, North American Aviation also submitted a design for this vehicle. Though it had no experience making rocket planes, it had built several ground breaking manned aircraft. Additionally, NAA's Navaho program had been gathering extensive data on flight at Mach 3 at altitudes over 60,000 feet. The Mach 3 wind tunnel at Santa Susanna gave it an important edge over the competition.

The use of Navaho data allowed North American to propose a superb design. Not only was the vehicle capable of flight over Mach 3, but Mach 5. North American also increased the flight altitude from over 60,000 feet to over 100,000 feet. In December of 1955 the Air Force accepted the design and construction began in 1956.

North American constructed three X-15s, the first flying in 1959. The three vehicles set many altitude and air speed records before the program ended in 1968. These records included an unofficial world speed record of Mach 6.7 and an altitude record of 314, 750 feet.

The first X-15 is in the Smithsonian Institutes National Air & Space Museum. The second is in the United States Air Force Museum at Wright-Patterson AFB [under the XB-70]. The third was lost during a flight on 15 November 1967 killing pilot Major Michael J Adams. A mockup of this aircraft is on display at Edwards AFB in memorial.

XB-70

The XB-70 was the first U.S. bomber to exceed Mach 3 in level flight. Today, it is still the largest supersonic aircraft ever flown. Its design features of a delta planform, twin tails and a forward canard show its Navaho heritage.

As noted in the text, the USAF launched the RISE vehicles specifically to gather data for the XB-70. Though the program ended after only two flights, their data – plus Fly-Five – produced an excellent database. Data on aeroheating, aero-elasticity, and particularly wave drag were instrumental in the development of this bomber. The work on wave drag resulted in the development of the compression lift principle.

Unfortunately, in the 1960s the U.S. Government replaced the high speed/high altitude bomber concept with the low altitude penetrator bomber. Research and development of the XB-70 bomber ended in 1962. The Air Force then transferred the two aircraft in construction to NASA for high speed research. The first aircraft then flew on 21 September 1964.

NASA tested the two XB-70s extensively. The aircraft routinely flew at speeds up to Mach 3 for periods of up to one hour. After the loss of aircraft number two in 1966 however, flight testing waned. Then in the winter of 1969 NASA retired the last XB-70 to Wright Patterson AFB.

An XB-70 takes off from the Edwards AFB runway. Here the Navaho delta canard planform is clearly visible. Internally, modular electronics and a huge flight control computer made the aircraft stable in flight. Its air intakes were variable converging/diverging types. It also had a large air conditioning system to keep the electronics [and the crew] cool during the high temperature Mach three flights. Photo by: Rockwell International.

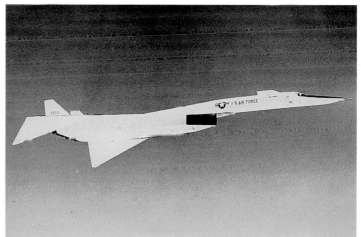

One aerodynamic advance NAA engineers made immediately after Navaho was the compressive lift principle. By lowering the XB-70s wing tips [as seen in this picture] the bomber could surf its own supersonic shock wave. The improved lift produced allowed the use of a smaller wing, reducing drag and increasing range. Due to its proximity to the Navaho time line. It's difficult to tell if this was developed independently of Navaho. Photo by: Rockwell International.

Today, any research into a supersonic transport starts with the data gathered in the XB-70 tests. And this data came from an aircraft developed from data gathered in the Navaho program. In some cases the XB-70 only verified the data gathered with the earlier G-26.

F-108

In many ways the North American Aviation F-108 looked more like a reduced size NAA A-5 Vigilante then a Navaho byproduct. The vehicle's planned 70,000 feet cruise altitude and Mach 3 cruise speed however were way beyond the A-5's performance. Thus, in this vehicle the Navaho legacy was internal.

Its aerodynamics showed the Navaho influence with its G-38 style full flying vertical tail. The aircraft also had variable converging/diverging engine inlets. These types of inlets would later be employed on such aircraft as the F-14 Tomcat and the F-15 Eagle.

Internally the aircraft was designed using Navaho material technology. Engineers made extensive use of Titanium and Aluminum honeycomb in the vehicles structure. The avionics also were developed from Navaho systems, particularly the transistor systems.

In many ways the F-108 was a competitor to the then secret Lockheed A-11/A-12 aircraft. Yet the vehicle had limited uses while Lockheed offered its aircraft in multiple versions. Thus on 23 September 1959 the Air Force canceled the program.

Aerodynamic Planform

Though none of the following aircraft were developed using Navaho aerodynamic data, they have similar aerodynamics. These aircraft show how far ahead of its time the X-10's full flying Delta/Canard planform was.

MiG-21

The first aircraft to have even remotely similar aerodynamics to the X-10 was the Russian MiG-21. This aircraft was a delta wing with a full flying rear horizontal stabilizer. This rear horizontal stabilizer distinguished the MiG-21 from the other delta wing aircraft of the 1950s: the Mirage, F-102 and F-106.

Like the forward canard, the rear horizontal allows the MiG-21 to achieve higher angles of attack on takeoff and during flight. This higher AOA produces higher lift, allowing the aircraft to use a smaller delta wing then a tailless delta design. A smaller wing means lower wing drag, and even with the drag created by the rear horizontal stabilizer, resulting in a net reduction in drag. Thus, the plane can fly farther and faster then aircraft of similar size and engine thrust.

The rear horizontal also is a convergent control surface. To cause the aircraft to pitch up, the rear horizontal is pitched down. This causes it to lose lift [or create negative lift] allowing the tail to drop. As the tail drops the nose pitches up and the main wing gains lift: the aircraft begins climbing. As the aircraft rotates up however, the rear horizontal also begins pitching upward in the airflow. Positive lift increases and the horizontal begins pushing the tail back up. This effect damps out the upward rotation producing stability.

On a canard aircraft, as the canard rotates upward lift increases. This in turn increases the pitching moment causing the aircraft to pitch up further and causing the canard to increase lift. On subsonic aircraft, eventually the canard stalls limiting pitch up to a specific angle. On a supersonic canard aircraft however, the canard never stalls. This means that the aircraft can actually pitch up and over and begin tumbling end-over-end in flight. This is why in 1956 only the PIX-10 autopilot could control the X-10 in supersonic flight.

A poor picture of a MiG-21 during take off. The MiG-21 was the first manned jet aircraft to have both a delta wing and a movable horizontal stabilizer. Its use of a independent horizontal allowed it to function with a smaller wing. The drag reduction this produced, coupled with the enhanced pitch response made the MiG-21 a deadly fighter in the 1950s and 1960s. Photo by: U.S. Department of Defense.

The MiG's horizontal stabilizer improves pitch control while allowing the aircraft to be aerodynamically stable. It is not unstable at supersonic speeds like the X-10, but it is bet-

A SAAB Viggen climbs above the clouds. The first manned fighter design to have both a delta wing and an adjustable canard, it is highly maneuverable. This later model JA-37 has been the main stay of the Swedish air defense forces since the 1970s. Before that the plane was Sweden's primary attack aircraft. Photo by: SAAB.

ter than a pure tailless delta design like the F-106. The first of these MiGs entered service in 1959. They are still flown by several third world Air Forces.

SAAB VIGGEN

The next aircraft was the Swedish Viggen. A true delta canard aircraft, but using a flapped canard like the XB-70 Valkyrie. It had greater aerodynamic potential then the MiG but not as much as the older X-10.

A replacement for the SAAB Draken delta wing aircraft, the Viggen began entering service in 1971. As expected, its canard allowed it to achieve higher angle-of-attacks then the Draken design. Thus, it could use shorter runways, and had superior maneuverability.

Though it had superior maneuverability to other jet aircraft, the Viggen did not have the full aerodynamic potential of the X-10 design. To limit the vehicle's aerodynamics enough to allow manned control, SAAB used a flapped canard instead of full flying. The canard also was moved back from the nose to just in front of the main wing's center of lift. This reduced the pitching moment produced by the canard, reducing the effect. The Viggen could still achieve high AOA's, but not as quickly as the X-10.

Three Israeli Kfirs in flight over the eastern Mediterranean. By adding canards to the basic Mirage design the Israelis produced a marked improvement in maneuverability. The new design was now more then a match for MiG-21s flown by then threatening Arab nations. Photo by: Israeli Aircraft Industries.

The position of the canard over the wing did give the Viggen an aerodynamic improvement not seen in the X-10 program. Tip vortices produced by the canard cancel similar vortices produced by the upper surface of the wing. This sta-

A Dassault Mirage III after its canard retrofit: the vehicle has yet to be painted. The aerodynamic improvements these fixed surfaces produce at subsonic speed are exceptional. Yet it took more then twenty years for Dassault learn what North American aerodynamicists knew in 1951. Photo by: Dassault Aviation, taken by J. L. Cardey.

bilization of the air flow allows for even higher angles-of-attack before the wing stalls [during subsonic flight]. To SAAB engineers this is called a super stall.[1]

The Viggen is still in service with the Swedish Air Force.

IAI Kfir C-2 And Spin-offs
The Israeli Kfir C-2 is an updated Dassault Mirage III, but with one special difference. To increase its maneuverability the Israelis added small fixed canards just forward and above the main wing. When the design entered service in July 1976 it had significantly improved AOA over the Mirage and the Kfir C-1.

In the years following the Kfir C-2, Dassault began fielding a canard upgrade kit for the Mirage III. According to Dassault, the addition of small fixed canards increases maximum low subsonic [Mach 0.3] Angle-Of-Attack [AOA] from 15 to 26 degrees. This low speed improvement allows for shorter runways and high pitch maneuverability in a dog fight. Low altitude turn rate also increased from 11 degrees per sec to 16 at 10,000 feet.

As one would expect however the improved maneuverability drops off as the vehicle increases speed. At Mach 0.75 the maximum AOA is only 19 degrees, the MAX AOA of a standard Mirage III. This aerodynamic limitation is partly due to the canard's position, partly due to it being fixed. The canards only slightly increase instability, not enough to make the vehicle uncontrollable by a human pilot in supersonic flight.

Recent Designs
Fly-By-Wire technology and the microprocessor has allowed

A Gripen mimics an earlier Viggen photo by climbing for altitude. The Gripen is the first manned supersonic aircraft to have an X-10 style full flying canard. It has taken thirty years, but our flight control technology has finally caught up with our aerodynamic knowledge. Photo by: SAAB Scandia.

the development of manned, supersonic aircraft with full flying canards like the X-10/G-26. These new software driven flight control computers are both more powerful and smaller than the X-10's computers. Linked in groups of three or more they give the reliability necessary to man rate such unstable planforms as the X-10's.

Gripen
In Sweden the first Gripen fighters are reaching Swedish Air Force units. The Gripen is everything the Viggen could have been if the flight control technology had been available. Its

full flying canard design is aerodynamically unstable, but the flight computers make it controllable. Like the Viggen however, the design is aerodynamically limited by the placement of the canard just in front of the main wing.

Though SAAB restrained the Gripen's aerodynamics, the aircraft has had flight control problems. Two aircraft have crashed due to problems with the system's software. The last crash was caused by the system being rate limited; this caused a divergent pilot-induce-oscillation [PIO].

A Rafale D sits on the taxiway, its canards pitched upward. The Rafale D has flight capabilities beyond that of the Mirage III and the Mirage 2000. Its canards give it exceptional maneuverability at both subsonic and supersonic speeds. The aircraft is being tested for use on French carriers where good landing maneuverability is a must. Photo by: Dassault Aircraft, taken by J. L. Cardey.

To correct these problems, SAAB is installing new software and computers. The new ADA based software includes a phase correcting filter to prevent PIO. The new Lockheed-Martin computers, four for each aircraft, are faster and more reliable. The Gripen's flight control system is quadruple redundant for reliability.

Rafale D
In France Dassault is testing its new delta/canard aircraft. The Rafale's canards primarily improve air flow over the upper surface of the wing. They are however full flying, producing active pitch control.

The Rafale is the most limited of the recent batch of delta canard aircraft. Its canards are the smallest and they are placed just above and in front of the wing. These aerodynamic limitations give it the lowest potential maneuverability of the new delta/canard aircraft. It also makes it the easiest to control.

Unlike the Gripen, the Rafale has not had any crashes due to pilot-induced oscillation or computer problems. Its design also allows it to fly with only three electronic computer flight control systems. A duel-channel analog system makes up a fourth unit, but it is only a backup system and is for subsonic flight.

The Rafale system shows some of the sophisticated computer capability necessary to control an unstable delta/canard aircraft. Its software is reported to have over 1.2 million lines of code.

LAVI
Israel also has produced a delta/canard design. The aircraft looks like a F-16XL delta wing fighter with a forward full flying canard. Research on this aircraft was curtailed in the 1990s

An Israeli LAVI in flight. Here again we have the delta/canard planform with the canard full flying. Though the program to develop a new Israeli fighter has been mothballed, the Peoples Republic of China is planning a version. By the year 2,000 this fighter will be flying against French Rafales and Swedish Gripens. Photo by: Israeli Aircraft Industries.

due to Israeli budget limitations. The program also was viewed as provocative in light of recent peace talks.

After several years in hiatus, in 1995 the People's Republic of China signed an agreement with Israel to build a stripped down version of this aircraft. Even stripped of its special ECM and ECCM systems, this aircraft will have one

A Eurofighter prototype in flight. The Eurofighter is the first of this next generation of delta canard designs to use the canard as a control surface. Like the X-10, the canard is far forward of the wing leading edge. This increases the pitching moment produced by the canards during flight, improving maneuverability. It also makes the vehicle more unstable. Photo By: British Aerospace.

of the more sophisticated flight control systems in the world. It also will be one of the most maneuverable fighters on the international market.

EuroFighter 2000

The Eurofighter is the last of the European delta canard aircraft in development. The first manned aircraft to have a planform similar to the X-10, it has exceptional maneuverability. This maneuverability exists at both subsonic and supersonic speeds [AOAs over 40 degrees].

Unlike the Gripen, Rafale and LAVI, the Euro 2000 has its full flying canard well forward of the main wing. This makes it a true flight control surface and not an air flow stabilization device. This also makes the aircraft more unstable and thus more dependent on its flight control system.

The Euro 2000 has quadruple flight control computers, quadruple control actuators, quad motion sensors, and quad pilot input sensors. Four Mil-Std 1553 Fly-By-Wire data buses and two 1773 fiberoptic data buses tie everything together. It is one of the most complication flight control systems in testing, all necessary to man rate this aircraft.

X-31

The last aircraft is the only one with even a slight connection with the Navaho program. The X-31 was developed jointly by Messerschmitt-Bolkom-Blohm and Rockwell International. Rockwell International bought out North American in the early 1970s.

The X-31 is the smallest and most agile of the delta canard aircraft in testing. Its full flying canard is far forward of

A Rockwell/MBB X-31 in flight over Edwards. The great-grandson of the X-10, this delta canard aircraft goes one better with vectored thrust. The combination of vectored thrust, full flying canard, and delta make this the most maneuverable aircraft in the world today. Photo by: Rockwell International.

the main wing giving the aircraft a strong pitching moment [Cm values of up to 0.6]. In tests the aircraft has achieved stable angle-of-attacks as high as 70 degrees to the vehicle's direction of flight. The X-31 is in fact the first aircraft to complete a Herbst maneuver.

The X-31 is a pure test aircraft, not a production prototype. With the loss of the first prototype due to icing of an air speed sensor, the remaining aircraft is finishing the test program. After that it will probably be sent to Wright-Patterson AFB were it will be stored next to its great grandfather, X-10 19307.

Miscellaneous
Materials

Because of the amount of titanium to be used in the G-38 wings, NAA worked with Titanium producers to develop new fabrication techniques. These techniques were later used in the construction of the Lockheed A-12 and SR-71 black birds.

The Navaho program also is reported to have been the source of bonded aluminum honeycomb. Today, this material is used throughout our aerospace industry: both civilian and military.

ChemMilling

ChemMill is one of the greatest gifts of the Navaho program. Like aluminum honeycomb and titanium, it is used throughout our aerospace industry to produce lightweight structural pieces. Its ability to sculpt integral structure into skin sections makes it a regular process in our aerospace industry. Its ability to reduce metal components down to the absolute bare minimum required regularly cuts significant amounts of weight from aircraft structure.

Arc Welding

Heli-arc Fusion welding of aluminum and stainless steel is another by-product of the Navaho program. Its uses go way beyond the aerospace industry to automobiles, ships, trains, etc.

Modular electronics

Though the Navaho program did not create the transistor it

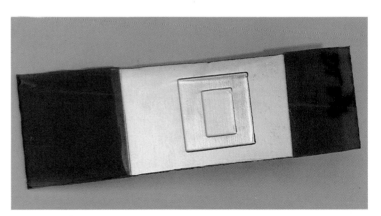

A sample of metal Chem-Milled to form a pattern. Such manufacturing technologies as Chem-Mill and Heli-Arc welding are still in use today. Navaho developed materials like Aluminum Honeycomb and Titanium are also mainstays of our nation's aircraft industry. Photo by: McDonnell-Douglas.

was one of the first users of it. Today transistorized electronics are in everything: cars, boats, trains, microwave ovens, electric razors, TVs and radios. Even the computer this book was written on uses similar transistors, diodes and capacitors to those used in the Navaho.

The revolutionary modular design of the Navaho's electronics also are standard today. The removal and replacement of individual circuit boards is normal repair procedures. Gone completely is the time consuming pattern of removing, testing, and replacing multiple vacuum tubes. This modular technology, coupled with the higher live spans of solid state electronics, has improved reliability [up time] .

Modular solid state electronics would take a decade to reach civilian consumers. In the years that have followed however, this technology coupled with the microprocessor [developed in the Apollo Moon program], would revolutionize the world.

NOTES

(1) Though not an aerodynamic issue, the canard was also placed behind the cockpit. This insured that it did not get in the way of the pilot's view of the runway during approach and landing.

Epilogue

The Navaho may have been a failure as a military weapon, but as a Research and development program it was spectacular. The technology it developed made American military systems the most powerful in the world for the next twenty years. A total of five strategic missile systems used key Navaho guidance and propulsion technology. Many more aircraft and missiles benefited from its advanced materials and modular electronics.

The Navaho program also served as a starting point for our space program. Again its propulsion technology, electronics and materials was used on practically all 1960s era U.S. space vehicles. Even today's Space Shuttle has been compared to the Navaho G-38 with its three gimballed rocket engines and piggy-back booster arrangement.

Yes, Never-Go-Navaho produced more aerospace spinoffs than any other missile or aircraft program. It truly has earned the name the Air Force has bestowed on it: The Know-how Missile. And so we end this book on the Navaho missile program. This is not a conclusion however, just an ending.

So much of the history of the Navaho program is still unpublished, due to lingering government controls. It may not be until the next century when all the documents about this program are free for publication.

In the same way the legacy of the Navaho is still growing. Aircraft and even new space vehicles use the materials and construction techniques developed for the G-38. Recently a new space vehicle called the X-34 was considering using the sustainer motor from an Atlas. And almost yearly some one proposes a super launch vehicle using Saturn V F1 engines. Thus, Navaho based engines will continue to be used in American space systems.

Like a pebble dropped down a mountain, dislodging new rocks as it goes, the Navaho legacy continues to grow. Also, in the years to come the government will release new facts on the missile's development. Thus, this history will continue to expand and improve until Navaho technology becomes as basic to Aerospace as the wheel.

Bibliography

The following is a listing of books, and publications that were used to research this manuscript. It is provided solely to give the readers an idea of the written sources used to produce this manuscript. Many of these documents and sources only recently became available.

Books

North American Aviation, Inc. *Structural and Manufacturing Summary, RTV-A-5 Airframe*. 15 March 1951. Declassified, October 1959

Chapman, John. *Atlas: The Story Of A Missile*. New York: Harper 1960.

Gunston, Bill. *Rockets and Missiles*. England: Leisure Books. 1979.

Hansen, Chuck. *US Nuclear Weapons, The Secret History*. New York: Orion Books 1988.

Hartt, Julian. *The Mighty Thor: Missile in Readiness*. New York: Duell 1961.

Miller, Jay. *The X-Planes, X-1 to X-29*. Minnesota: Specialty Press. 1983

Neufeld, Jacob. *Ballistic Missiles in the United States Air Force: 1945-1960*. Office of Air Force History, United States Air Force, Washington, DC. 1990.

Werrell, Kenneth P. *The Evolution Of The Cruise Missile*, Maxwell AFB: Air University Press. 1985.

Yenne, Bill. *Rockwell, The Heritage of North American*. Greenwich: Crescent Books. 1989

Pace, Steve. *X-Fighters*, Motorbooks International. 1991

Chronologies

Weapon System 104A: HISTORICAL SUMMARY. Missile Division, North American Aviation, Inc. MD 59-247, 8 June 1959.

Thirty-Five Years in Power for America: A History of the Rocketdyne Division of Rockwell International. Rocketdyne Division of Rockwell Int. Pages 10-13.

Navaho - Weapon System 104-A, Prepared by Supervisory Training, North American Aviation, 14 June 1967.

Major Milestones, NR Space Division History, 1945 to 1970. North American Rockwell, Space Division. By R.B. Oakley

A Chronology Of Missile And Astronautic Events (1962)

Air Force Missile Test Center History, 1 January-30 June 1952, pp 285-286.

Air Force Missile Test Center History, 1 January-30 June 1953, pp 130.

Air Force Missile Test Center History, 1 July-31 December 1953, pp 278-323.

Air Force Missile Test Center History, 1 January-30 June 1954, pp 173-178.

Air Force Missile Test Center History, 1 July-31 December 1954, pp 283-286

Air Force Missile Test Center History, 1 January-30 June 1955, pp 410-411

Air Force Missile Test Center History, 1 July-31 December 1955, pp 258-322

Air Force Missile Test Center History, 1 January-30 June 1956, pp 55, 181-191

Air Force Missile Test Center History, 1 July-31 December 1956, pp 176-185

Air Force Missile Test Center History, 1 January-30 June 1957, pp 170-181.

Air Force Missile Test Center History, 1 July-31 December 1957, pp 166-169

Air Force Missile Test Center History, 1 January-30 June 1958, pp 142-144

Air Force Missile Test Center History, 1 July-31 December 1958, pp 161-164

Air Force Missile Test Center History, 1 January-30 June 1959, pp 158-159.

Fact Sheets/Documents

Standard Missile Characteristics, North American X-10. By Authority of the Secretary of the Air Force. Published, prior to 1956. Classification changed to unclassified 8 July 1968.

XSM-64 FLIGHT TEST SUMMARY. Missile Development Division, North American Aviation, Inc, 10 February 1958.

X-10 Flight Test Program, Summary of Completed Flights. Report No. AL-1471, North American Aviation. Page 4.50.02 Revised 6-15-55.

X-10 Flight Test Program, Summary of Remaining Flights. Report No. AL-1471, North American Aviation. Page 4.50.00, Revised 6 15 55.

The personal notes of Joe Pomykata of the first nine X-10 flights.

Booster-Static Test #1, Pictures After Failure. North American document. Personal momento of W. F. Gibson Jr.

Articles

Murray, Russ. "*The Navaho Inheritance*." American Aviation Historical Society Journal, Spring 1974, Volume 19, PP 17-21

Murray, Russ. "*Downey Plant, Cradle of the Cosmic Age*." Rockwell International Public Affairs.

Meyers, Dale D. "*The Navaho Cruise Missile - A Burst Of Technology*." Acta Astronautica, 1992, Volume 26 No. 8-10, pp 741-748.

Downey Skywriter, North American Aviation, Inc. 1 Nov 1957, Vol XVII, No. 44.

Downey Skywriter, North American Aviation, Inc. 1 Feb 1957, Vol XVIII, No. 5.

Downey Skywriter, North American Aviation, Inc. 28 Feb 1958, Vol XVIII, No. 9

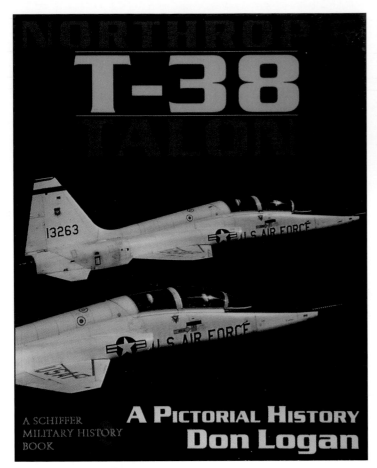

NORTHROP'S T-38 TALON
A PICTORIAL HISTORY

Don Logan

This is the story of the most successful pilot training jet ever produced: the Northrop T-38 Talon. All units flying the T-38, their markings and paint schemes are covered in over 300 color photographs – including a chart of the colors used listing Federal Standard (FS) color numbers.
Size: 8 1/2" x 11" over 300 color photographs
152 pages, soft cover
ISBN: 0-88740-800-1 $24.95

ONE-OF-A-KIND RESEARCH AIRCRAFT
A History of In-Flight Simulators,
Testbeds & Prototypes

Steve Markman & Bill Holder

Covered are: Inflight Simulation Aircraft; VISTA/NF-16D; NC-131H Total In-Flight Simulator; Testbed Aircraft; F-8 Supercritical Wing; F-15 AECS; F-15 ASAT; F-15 Streak Eagle; F-16 AFTI; F-16 CCV, FLOTRAK; F/A-18 EPAD; F/A-18 HARV; Prototype Aircraft; YA-7F (A-7 Plus); F-16XL; F-16/79/101; P-51 Mustang-Based Enforcer; Gunships; F-15E Strike Eagle Demonstrator, and many others.
Size: 8 1/2" x 11" over 200 color and b/w photographs
152 pages, hard cover
ISBN: 0-88740-797-8 $45.00